Good

and

Faithful Servant

Patty Old West

YorkshirePublishing
www.yorkshirepublishing.com
Write Now.

ISBN: 978-1-950034-19-2
Good and Faithful Servant
Copyright © 2019 by Patty Old West

Unless otherwise noted, scripture quotations are taken from the *Holy Bible, King James Version,* Cambridge, 1769.

Scripture quotations marked 'NEB' are from *The New English Bible,* The Delegates of the Oxford University Press and the Syndics of the Cambridge University Press, 1961, 1970.
Poetry excerpts are from *Footprints in the Dust* by Kenneth G. Old.

For permission requests, write to the publisher at the address below.

Yorkshire Publishing
4613 E. 91st St,
Tulsa, OK 74137
www.YorkshirePublishing.com
918.394.2665

Good

and

Faithful Servant

the extraordinary life of Ken Old in Pakistan

"Well done, **good and faithful servant**
you were faithful over a few things,
I will make you ruler over many things.
Enter into the joy of your lord."
Matthew 25:23

Patty Old West

Contents

Acknowledgements

This book has been long in the planning. The initial chapters were written while Ken was still alive so he could verify the details of his early life. Many others gave quite generously of their time in editing this book.

The initial manuscript was reviewed by my three darling daughters, Sandy Gaudette, Becky Shupe, and Karin Spanner. Their proofreading corrected many errors. My dear friends, Rick and Kay Janecke, offered some good suggestions. And I am grateful to them for their gentle and loving support. Patty Wilburn, bless her heart, was instrumental in helping me separate the chaff from the wheat. Another good friend, Glenda Schlahta took time from her busy schedule to review the manuscript. Her suggestions fine-tuned the book further.

With gratitude and appreciation, I extend my heartfelt thanks to these wonderful people who have been such and encouragement to me.

Preface

Kenneth George Old was the second child in a family of ten children. He began life in a small village in Cornwall. A man of many talents, multi-faceted in interests and accomplishments, he styled himself as, 'Just an ordinary man'. If so, he was an ordinary man with a difference. The difference, of course, was due to the fact that he was a man who loved the Lord with his whole heart. An encounter with God in 1949 led to him promising God that He could have the rest of his life to use in whatever way He saw fit. It was a promise that he kept and never swerved from. For Ken, choices were always made based on the purposes of God.

Ken's accomplishments included working in the Admiralty Building in London. It was the beginning of World War II and he delivered decoded enemy messages. Later, he was the only officer in charge of a German concentration camp. After the war he was involved in the Thames River project. God directed him to Pakistan where he constructed cement factories, hospital operating blocks, village schools, and church roofs.

Ken and his first wife, Marie spent 35 years as missionaries in Pakistan loving the people and keeping their home open to volunteers and visitors from around the world. None went away the same person as before. Ken had the privilege of supervising the Christian Technical Training Center for boys the last 20 years of his time in Pakistan. For his work in community development and education he was awarded an OBE. This is an honor bestowed by the Queen granting him 'the Dignity of an Ordinary Officer of the British Empire'.

He could claim friendship with notables around the world while maintaining a special rapport with small children. He was famous among the missionary children for his stories of the Little People. These stories were first told to the children living at boarding school away from their parents. The loneliest children became the heroes of that evening's episode.

One of his close friends was Bilquis (Bill-keese) Sheik (Shake) who wrote the story of her life in 'I Dared to Call Him Father'. The inscription in the first edition gift copy she gave to Ken reads:

> To Dearest Ken and Marie,
>
> With everlasting gratitude to God for giving me perfect friends, through whom I learnt much, and will always do, as a teacher and guide of deep spiritual knowledge. This book has become possible because of Ken's message from God that it should be written.
>
> I love you both very much.
>
> Bilquis Sheikh 24.12.1978

Although Ken was accomplished in so many different aspects of life, he maintained a simple trust in God. His wasn't a blind faith, for he was always questioning, but there was never any doubting involved in his questioning.

Ken told many stories of how God worked in providing resources—enormous amounts—to finance building work and provide food for an entire orphanage that he and Marie were running. God intervened in perilous circumstances by removing guards at a gate that was always heavily guarded around the clock. Other times He gave clear direction in an audible voice. He was instructed to go see a person 200 miles away! And God was specific answering prayer. Ken prayed for the car to stop at a fixed place to determine if he should ask Marie to marry him. He wasn't driving, but it did!

God's provision of the old Tudor farmhouse in Sellindge meant that Ken was blessed so he could be a blessing to others. This home, like the one in Pakistan, was open to visitors from around the world. The perfect peace and gracious hospitality provided rest and renewal of spirit for those fortunate enough to find their way to its door.

This volume is an attempt to portray what a truly extraordinary and remarkable man Ken really was.

St. Newlyn East

C ornwall. The young saplings drive their roots deeper to keep from being swept away by fierce winds howling across the west coast from the Atlantic. They may be as stubborn as any Cornishman, but they can't grow straight. The angle caused by the constant determined buffeting of forceful gales will continue as they mature. On one such cold, windy day, the 2nd of May, 1925, a little old lady struggles to keep her balance as she makes her way to the center of town for her daily shopping. Suddenly, sounds of lusty cries from a newborn babe waft through the air from the room above the green-doored shop opposite. Smiling sweetly, she wonders—"What kind of life lies ahead for the child?"

Kathleen, only 20, has already given birth to her first-born son, Joe. The one-year-old now has a brother, Kenneth George, so named by his father. His middle name, in remembrance of Granny George, recently deceased, will also serve to honor the Patron Saint of England. Richard will keep this idea in mind to honor saints of the United Kingdom for any future children.

The family lives in the village of St. Newlyn East about five miles south of Newquay. At one time it was a thriving mining community. The word 'Montana' painted above the door of the shop indicates money had been sent from abroad by one of the locals who had gone to America to seek his fortune in the copper mines of Butte. It had become increasingly unprofitable to keep the tin mines in operation—the last of them closed in 1881. Many of the hardworking miners took their expertise to the Rocky Mountains. Many ended up in Central City, Colorado, known as 'the richest square mile on earth' for its gold mines.

The village has a 'Pit' which is used for special occasions such as tea treats— the Cornish version of a picnic. It was built after a disaster at the East Wheal Rose mine claimed 39 lives. This disaster wasn't a cave-in. The mine was actually flooded by an unusually heavy thunderstorm and the miners were drowned. The surviving miners, thankful their own lives had been spared, dug the 'Pit' as a memorial.

The village is named after St. Newlyna, the female saint uniquely associated with this close-knit hamlet. The first recording of her is from 1259. Tradition says she came from Ireland. Landing at Holywell, she walked to the spot where the church now stands. Thrusting her staff into the ground, she declared,

"Let a church be built here." And so it was. It has become the focal point that gives purpose to the town. The famous fig tree growing out of the wall next to the massive wooden double doors of the church is said to have come from her staff. The interior of the beautiful old Anglican Church is cross shaped, measuring about 45 feet wide with three-foot-thick walls. The massive short granite columns with bases and capitals of enormous size give the church the appearance of a much older building. St. Newlyna is believed to have been the daughter of a king who beheaded her with his own hands because of her refusal to marry the man of his choosing. Fragments of a 15th century cross are said to represent a female figure carrying her own head, which is thought to be St. Newlyna.

The gardens surrounding the church contain many unique plants which are of interest to gardening enthusiasts. The ancient yew tree, found in nearly every churchyard, keeps watch over headstones inscribed with the name Daw, ancestors of little Kenneth George. The pathway leading to the church is lined on each side with headstones that are silent testimonies to the transition of time. They no longer mark graves, but merely acknowledge the life that once was. Across the road are the local butcher and sweet shops, closed up tight on a Sunday as all shops once were.

Cornwall is the heart of John Wesley country. Methodist chapels and churches are sprinkled liberally over the countryside. St. Newlyn boasts two chapels in regular use and a third that now sits idle, plus a church for the tiny village, having a mere few hundred residents.

One traditional Cornish food is the pasty. Pronounced 'passtee', it's a simple meat pie transformed into a purer and more idealized form. It was a convenient way to provide nourishment with a rich, delicious taste to the hungry miners. Upon opening his lunch box, a man would fondly refer to it as "a letter from home." There is an art to making a good pasty. The subtle intricacies go beyond just following the recipe and have been handed down from mother to daughter for generations. Here, however, is the basic recipe:

Cornish Pasty

For Pastry:	For Filling:
1 lb. flour	1 lb. best quality lean beef
5 oz. lard	1 lb. potatoes
pinch of salt	1 lb. swede
water to mix	1 small onion (optional)
1 oz. butter	pepper and salt to taste

The finer quality the beef and the more finely cut the vegetables, the tastier will be the pasty.

Set oven to 400F or Mark 6. Make the pastry and divide into four equal pieces. Roll each piece into a round 7 inches in diameter. Cut up the potatoes into small, irregular shaped pieces, similarly the swede (and onion if used). Cut the beef into small cubes about 1/4-inch square, removing all fat. On each round of pastry put a share of the vegetables and add the salt and pepper to taste. Then add the meat and a knob of butter and another sprinkle of pepper. Dampen the edges of the pastry and bring up from both sides with floured hands to envelope the filling. Pinch the edges together and crimp them firmly to seal. Cook on a floured tray for 15 minutes. Makes four pasties.

Ken always judges a 'good' pasty by the way the potatoes are cut. His mother sliced them paper thin. In his opinion, cubed potatoes don't give the pasty the proper taste.

Newquay

THE CENTRAL ART GALLERY GOVER STREET, NEWQUAY, CORNWALL
(BETWEEN BARCLAY'S BANK AND THE TOWN BEACH.)
INSPECTION INVITED

Newquay today is a bustling tourist town. Known as the surfing capital of Europe for its magnificent waves, the once quiet main street is now crowded with young tanned bodies jostling for space. Loud music blares from the stores and bright flashing neon signs light up the night. Every corner shop sells or rents wetsuits, boards and the associated paraphernalia needed by the serious surfer.

In Newquay's early history the main source of income was fishing. The fishermen, however, didn't go out day after day with vain hopes of success. Instead, they had one man who lived in the Huer's Hut on an outcropping high above the sea. His job was to keep a sharp lookout for schools of fish. When he spotted them, he let out a 'hue and cry' to alert all the fishermen to get down to their boats. The story is told that the 'hue and cry' went out one Sunday morning during the church service, but not a single fisherman stirred until the sermon was over. The Huer's hut still stands on the outcropping, but is no longer in use.

Before Ken's family moves the five miles into Newquay from St. Newlyn East, a beautiful baby girl joins the family. Remembering his idea to honor the saints of the United Kingdom, Richard has named her Patricia as the feminine form of St. Patrick to represent Ireland. However, she's called by her middle name, Jean. It isn't long before precious little Patricia Jean has her father firmly wrapped around her little finger. When Jean enters school, the two brothers, keenly aware of their responsibility, make sure no harm befalls her.

Their first home in Newquay is at Quintrell Downs. Later they live off the backside of Trenance Hill above the Gannel Valley. The school on Crantock Street is a good mile or so away from home, but when the tide is out, the journey home often more than doubles. Mother knows by the state of the tides just where her children might be and why they are so late.

In those days there wasn't any fear in parents for their children, just a hope they weren't getting into trouble. Joe and Ken, and sometimes Jean with them, wandered all the way past Dad's shop down to Towan Beach, around and through the various beach and rock pools, on to the Great Western Beach and then back up the cliff on the far side before making their way to the front door where the smell of freshly baked yeast buns greets them. They don't often go as far as Tolcarne—and never with Jean.

There are further diversions to entertain them. Their meandering trail home now snakes past the railway station, where

Uncle Reg works as a porter. He nearly always has chocolate treats for them. They might possibly see Uncle Joe waiting for passengers and get a short ride in his cart. Then it's on to the stables where Grampa keeps his pair of carriage horses. He asks them about school and entertains his dawdling grandchildren with stories while grooming the glistening animals or polishing their leathers and horse brasses.

Newquay holds many memories for Ken. Heading down the hill towards school in the morning he passes by his grandparent's house. Invariably Granny Old is out on the porch watching for him to come by. She calls out, "Laddie, have ye had the use of your bawls taday?" The youngster is never quite sure what she's asking, but he knows if he answers, "Yes", she will send him on his way to school. If he says, "No", Granny quickly orders him inside. She takes down a tin from above the kitchen sink and puts a large dose of Andrew's Liver Salts in a glass of water. The fizzy drink isn't to his liking, but it's always followed by one of granny's tasty yeast buns, and that helps make the treatment a bit more tolerable.

The family continues to grow, and money is always a precious commodity. Ken's teacher, Mr. Bennetto, is aware of the struggle of many of the impoverished Newquay families as the Depression hits. One day, Ken manages to achieve a 100 percent on an arithmetic test, and this sympathetic teacher gives him sixpence. This is a tidy sum, and the boy feels like he's a millionaire! When he shows it to his mother, she heaves a sigh of relief. "God answers prayers!" It's exactly the amount she needs for butter, and she sends Ken off immediately to buy it. He's so proud that he can use his own money for it.

Ken's father works initially as an assistant to the blind owner of a Newquay art gallery. This is where he learns his trade. He occasionally visits parts of Europe with 'Boss Walker'.' Later, Richard manages his own art gallery in Gover Lane in Newquay. But the blind man isn't forgotten. Ken makes a point of stopping by on a regular basis after school to sit with and read to Mr. Walker.

Inevitably the walls of their home are covered with copies of paintings by old masters and French impressionists mixed with those by local Cornish artists. Ken and his siblings are getting a homeschool education in art. They learn an appreciation for fine art and what to look for that gives a painting quality. Ken can distinguish different styles, and he can identify the artist even though he may not have previously seen that particular painting. Kathleen tires of the profusion of frames on every wall and removes several when her husband is away. But as soon as Richard returns and sees empty wall space, the art gallery at home restarts and the spaces are quickly filled once again.

One day on his circuitous route home from Crantock Street School, Ken and a friend pass by the sweet shop. They stop to look in the window and point out the tempting confections they would buy if they had the money. Passing the alley next to the store, they notice a discarded box that still contains delicious looking candies. A whole box of chocolates has been carelessly tossed in the garbage can. Retrieving this precious box seems to Ken like stealing, but after all, it has obviously been thrown away, even if by mistake. He plans to take it home to share with his brothers and sister. But of course he and his friend must each have at least one before that. The anticipation of the smooth, rich taste of real chocolate, a rare treat for them, makes his mouth water. First, he offers one to his equally eager pal, and then chooses one for himself. Biting carefully into the luscious-looking candy to avoid losing any of a possible soft center, the joy suddenly turns sour. His face is screwed up in disbelief and disappointment with a bit of frustration mixed in. It isn't candy at all! It's an imitation look-alike, papier-mache designed for display in the window where real chocolate would soon melt. Although the chocolate wasn't even real, he never loses the guilt feeling of taking something that didn't belong to him.

Ken is the acknowledged master of choosing the right chestnut. Not for roasting, but for a game of Conkers. Carefully, one of the right size and weight must be chosen to withstand the onslaught of battering from multiple opponents. The selected horse chestnut is drilled with a small hole. A string is pulled through the hole, transforming the small future tree into a weapon for battle. Two players face each other, standing about four feet apart. Swinging the conker, the goal is to hit the opponent's weapon hard enough to break it. The player with the broken conker is out, and another steps in to face the champion. Ken's conker once withstood 120 hits before finally breaking. Ken decides to save another of his prize conkers to use the following year. Wondering how it might best be preserved, he decides it will do well if he hides it in the water tank. Upon retrieving it nearly 12 months later, he discovers it has dissolved, leaving a mucky mess in the tank. He never does tell his mother what he did.

One summer holiday the school arranges an outing to a manufacturer of railway passenger cars on the other side of the world. Well, to a small boy of eight, Swindon might as well be on the other side of the world. Such noisy excitement as the brown and cream passenger car chugs northeast full of bouncing children. They are on an adventure such as they have never experienced. At the end of the ride, they take a long walk through corridors to the vast cavernous shops where the passenger cars are being built. Wonderful new images assail them from every side. It's a long day with a pasty packed for lunchtime nourishment along the way. But a day designed to live on in their memories forever.

How Ken manages to save three pence is unknown, but save it he does, and he uses it to buy a *surprise* for his mother. Even as a child, his imagination is over-active. Beaming with delight, handing over the precious savings to the clerk, he leaves with his prize possession tucked away safely in his pocket. Upon arriving home, he waits until his mother, her back turned to him, is busy at the kitchen sink. Removing the present from his pocket, he places it carefully on the floor and lets it go. A whir and a scream! Kathleen first jumps sideways, and then lunges towards Ken as the mechanical mouse careens around the kitchen. Ken chuckles over it for years to come.

Quite often, on his straggling way home from school, Ken will play along the lower cliffs on the headland. The cliffs above the bay extend high above the sea. Up on the cliff, one can look out across the Atlantic Ocean toward distant unseen lands thousands of miles away. The waves crash against the cliffs with unbelievable force. A small boy looking out on the tumbling waves at sunset can imagine exciting adventures among the clouds.

Playing in the 'tea caverns' under the cliffs, Ken fantasizes he is part of a smuggler gang unloading kegs of tea into the caves. This is tricky business. Not only is the footing slippery, but becoming too engrossed in play and forgetting to watch the incoming tides can leave one trapped. There's no possibility of swimming against the tide to escape from the cave. Wisdom demands heading for home at first sight of rising water.

During one fantasy playtime, Ken and two or three of his friends are unloading contraband as Preventive Officers look for them just the other side of the rocks. Another school friend, wanting to join them in a hurry, decides to slide down the steep cliff instead of taking the path. Wilburforce hits a tuft of grass and tumbles head over heels landing in a crumpled heap at the bottom. The startled boys dash up the hill to the Atlantic Hotel for help. A stream of staff and guests quickly follow them back to the cliff-side to rescue the fallen boy. Ken runs all the way home. His lungs are bursting as he arrives. His mother is just taking a batch of yeast buns from the oven as he comes flying in with the news. Stopping only briefly to leave his shoes at the door, he gulps down that first bun so necessary to keeping a starving child alive. His mother is waiting to hear what has happened that has so upset her son.

On the lane between Indian Queens and Newquay there's a spot near White Cross where the coastal town can be seen in the distance three or four miles away. One day as Ken walks towards Newquay from Fraddon, he meets an old man seated on a bench. It's time for a rest. Conversation reveals the man lives nearby. Ken points towards Newquay and asks, "Do ye go to Newquay often then?"

The man replies, "Went thur once when I wuzz a boy. Didn't

like it. Never been back since." Ken thinks, 'What a terrible waste of a life. He's missing out on enjoying new experiences.'

Sidcup, Kent

At the end of 1934, the Depression has forced the family to move from the Cornish Coast up to Kent, where they settle in Sidcup to the southeast of London. Richard's business as an art dealer hasn't survived the economic crisis. In order to feed the growing family, now numbering four boys and three girls, he becomes a commercial traveler selling art reproductions.

For Ken, now nine, it's a world far removed from the beaches and the sounds of the sea and seagulls. One of the things he misses most is the excitement of a lifeboat being launched and then returning through the town to the Lifeboat House.

Still the wanderer, Ken wends his way home along a lane between the Infants School and Days Lane, past an orchard where an old barn is being torn down. Before it is completely dismantled, he climbs up into the beams in the roof. To his amazement, he finds a bird's nest, still occupied. Newly hatched birds are waiting for the mother bird to return with fresh food. All he can see are mouths narrowly rimmed by colored beaks— no bodies, only half a dozen gaping mouths. It's a striking image that in later years, he uses to illustrate verse 10 in Psalm 81— 'Open your mouth wide and I will fill it.'

Even though Ken feels Joe is a lot smarter, Ken is the first in his family to be granted a scholarship to the County School, the local grammar school. His mind is always taking flights of fantasy, and in his first year there he is 11th in his class. There are only eleven students in the class. By the time he graduates in 1941 he is about fourth.

Ken's parents find it hard to make ends meet. School uniforms are required. It's an expense that requires digging deep into slender pockets. Joe is able to leave school at fourteen and works to earn money for the family. Ken walks to school each day to avoid paying bus fare. It's a four-mile journey that saves a whole penny. As he grows older, he helps out by taking on morning and evening newspaper deliveries. He also delivers milk and bread. On rare occasions, he splurges and spends a half-penny on some treats at the corner shop halfway home from school.

Midway through his morning newspaper route, he stops to read the headline news before carefully placing that newspaper on the customer's porch. In order to read comic strips, he stops at the last house and leans against the lamppost while the householder, watching through his window, waits patiently.

He's still delivering newspapers in the summer of 1940 while the Battle of Britain rages. The skies swarm with vapor trails of massed German planes. There are sounds of anti-aircraft fire, and the bouncing on the ground of falling shell splinters!

Two practices from Ken's school days last him a lifetime and give him much enjoyment over the years. One is the requirement to memorize both poetry and passages of Scripture. 70 years later he can still recite many poems first learned in grade school. The other is the singing of hymns during assembly each morning. He stands tall and straight, shoulders back, singing earnestly with firm determination 'To Be a Pilgrim.'

To Be a Pilgrim

Who would true valour see,
Let him come hither;
One here will constant be,
Come wind, come weather;
There's no discouragement
Shall make him once relent
His first avowed intent
To be a pilgrim.
Whoso beset him round
With dismal stories
Do but themselves confound;
His strength the more is.
No lion can him fright;
He'll with a giant fight;
But he will have a right
To be a pilgrim.
Hobgoblin nor foul friend
Can daunt his spirit;
He knows he's at the end
Still life inherit.

Then fancies fly away,
He'll fear not what men say;
He'll labour night and day
To be a pilgrim.

The Essential Bombe

By the time Ken leaves the County School at 16 the night bombing has become routine. For two years he commutes into London to work alternate night and day shifts with the War Registry in the Admiralty Building. Working with the teams decoding enemy messages, he is keenly aware of the critical nature of the conflict going on at sea.

The German military uses a cipher machine called *Enigma*. Being able to decipher *Enigma* messages is particularly important as it provides the British Royal Air Force with valuable clues on the strength and organization of attacking Luftwaffe forces. It also reveals their intended targets. To crack the *Enigma* codes, the British Tabulating Machine Company builds 16 machines called Bombes. Each Bombe is about six feet high, six feet long, two feet deep and weighs close to a ton. All but the earliest have 36 sets of three rotors. Connections are tested at a rate of 100 times a second and when a match is found, the machine stops. One of the operators, usually a WREN (a member of the **W**omen's **R**oyal **N**aval **S**ervice), writes down the 'stop' value and sets the Bombe to running again. With the Bombe, *Enigma* keys can often be cracked in a few hours. It isn't ever a cut-and-dried operation, however, and obtaining success takes judgment, cleverness, skill, and... a bit of luck.

It is then Ken's responsibility to deliver the vital information to its destination as quickly as possible. Another of his assignments is finding filed messages urgently needed by his superiors. This can be quite challenging as the messages aren't always filed correctly and he has to look through several drawers before he finds the one needed. His shifts are 24 hours on and 24 hours off so he makes use of the free time to enjoy the theater—sitting 'among the gods' in the high balcony seats where the tickets are cheaper. Always curious, Ken climbs to the roof of the Admiralty Building during nighttime lunch breaks to get a better view of the bombs falling like fireworks all around London.

In April 1942 Germany retaliates for RAF raids on German cities. The Luftwaffe campaign targets significant English cities listed in the Baedeker Guide. Among these are Exeter, Bath, Canterbury, and York. More than 19,000 buildings are damaged or destroyed, and more than 400 people are killed.

Stimulated by the intensity of the war raging in Europe, Ken—now 18—decides to join the Army. Joe has already enlisted in the Air Force.

The government foresees a shortage of engineer officers for the Armed Services and introduces a civilian training scheme for potential engineer officers for the Royal Electrical and Mechanical Engineers. This takes Ken to Lincoln for a three-year course involving both academics and practical work experience.

In June 1944 a new threat appears in the skies. Londoners hesitate in their steps to listen to the buzzing of the 'doodle bugs'—so named because they sound like an Australian insect. As long as they continue to make noise, it's safe. Once they go quiet, it means an impact is imminent and it's necessary to take cover immediately. The air raid sirens whine incessantly. Ten thousand V-1 flying bombs are launched 130 miles from Germany to England. 2,419 of them reach London, killing over 6,000 people and injuring nearly 18,000. It's during such a time as this that Ken's youngest brother, Chris, is born in an air raid shelter. His father had given his fourth son the middle name of David in honor of St. David of Wales. Now for his tenth child, he uses Andrew to honor St. Andrew, the Patron Saint of Scotland. It is added, unbeknownst to Kathleen, to the already chosen names of Christopher Stanley. This is the last of his children, and completes the recognition of the saints of the United Kingdom as well.

India

In January 1946 Ken completes the intensive course of training as an Engineering Cadet at Lincoln University. The war has already ended. No longer are engineer officers needed. Ken is given a choice of three places to be sent— Singapore, Japan, or India. His first choice is Japan and then Singapore. Instead, he finds himself posted to India. He loves it passionately from the moment he arrives on the troopship in Bombay and sees the crowded trains in the dock sidings. Not only are people hanging out of the doors and windows, but many are sitting, ready for the journey, on the roofs of the trains.

It's a fascinating new world, teeming with people of different customs and several different faiths. He wants to know as much as he can about them.

The train ride on the Frontier Mail from near Poona (Pune) in India takes him through Delhi and Lahore to Rawalpindi. He's in company with a group of raw young British officers heading to Northern Army Headquarters for posting.

Lahore is the most depressing city Ken has seen so far in India. Along the railway tracks are shacks, hardly fit for animals, congested with people of all ages, sizes, and shapes, squatting in and near them. There's the filth and stench of the undesirable parts of a great city. Rawalpindi is Paradise by comparison.

The colonel has in his hand a list of cities where these new recruits will be sent. "Gentlemen, we have to sort out your postings. There are a few good places—Lahore, Quetta, Karachi, and Multan. It's no good my filling the good ones first so I'll start with the bad ones. There are two for Waziristan, anyone interested to go there?" He doesn't sound hopeful for volunteers. So his eyebrows rise when Nobby Newton and Ken shoot their hands up. They have absolutely no idea where Waziristan is, but they think it must be at the opposite end of the list to Lahore and that's good enough. Nobby goes to Bannu in North Waziristan and Ken is sent to Wana, in South Waziristan.

Wana is the major military garrison about 200 miles south of the Khyber Pass. This is tribal territory and not a settled area. The garrison lies on the territorial border of two of the fiercest of the Pathan tribes—the Wazirs and the Mahsuds. These are the ancestors of the modern day Taliban. The Mahsuds are slightly smaller in stature than the Wazirs, but they are equally courageous and equally feared. Ken's bodyguards come from these two tribes. Fifteen from each tribe will escort Ken and his staff to inspect roads and bridges, and the four outlying forts deep in tribal territory.

Ken's ultimate destination is the large fort at the end of a stony plain in the Northwest Frontier Province. The great military garrison at Wana was built between the wars. Vast quantities of cement were used in making the 8" x 8" x 16" concrete blocks for the walls and buildings. There's a long concrete runway to facilitate the rapid movement of troops if ever the very vulnerable road in or out should be blocked. The British have chosen Wana as the key location for the defense of the whole of India. Afghans and Russians, as well as local tribesmen, are all potential threats to peace.

Ken immediately falls in love with the barren wild country and its people. The Pathans are the world's largest tribal grouping, probably about 18 million in all. There are over 60 tribes spread over northwest India and Afghanistan. In the south, they speak a soft Pushtu, and in the north, a hard guttural Pukhtu. Most Pathans are Sunni Muslims. This gives Ken his first opportunity to watch their religion at work. He learns that Islam is the second most influential religion in the world and the second largest in the UK after Christianity. Its essence, its teaching influence all of life, both at home and work, and in interaction with others.

The ten months Ken spends in Waziristan fly by. He receives commendation from his superior officer:

> Mr. K.G. Old served under me as a Lieutenant in the Royal Engineers for a period of ten months during 1947. He was employed as an Assistant Garrison Engineer in the North West Frontier Province.
>
> I found Mr. Old a most energetic young man, hardworking, and capable of adapting himself to all conditions and emergencies with a sound knowledge of Engineering.
>
> During an operation with Tribesmen he displayed good courage and kept a cool head.
>
> Major R.L. Coveney R.E.

For some time, behind the scenes, negotiations have been going on that will forever change the country Ken has grown to love so much.

A year previously, a huge crowd of Mahsud and Wazir tribesmen gathered when Lord Wavell, the Viceroy of India, and Pandit Nehru flew in to address them about possible plans for India without the British. Those plans had not received a warm welcome. That one event, the inevitable and less costly alternative to civil war, has been bought at a terrible price. The cost isn't yet paid, but already its immensity is glimpsed.

On April 14, 1947, the details of the border line in the Punjab and Bihar / Bengal are delivered to the two Prime Ministers of India and the new Pakistan. On this day the province is still in India, but from midnight on it will be in Pakistan. The border with Afghanistan is somewhere in the hills beyond the west end of the plain, but there are only tracks and no motorable roads that give one reason to explore there.

Ten million people will be uprooted from their homes and lands occupied by their forbearers for centuries. Their fury at the decisions regarding their future is nothing to the fury and the terror and the tragedy that will be unleashed as the details become known across India. Lives depend on which side of the street a line is drawn. Many will find themselves in desperate flight before it's too late for anything except death. Reports claim that four million people lost their lives, although perhaps the true number is closer to half of that. What these figures actually mean is that families and neighbors and friends are turned into bitter enemies almost overnight. The everlasting immensity of this is utterly incomprehensible.

This is the last day for an age-old ceremony to take place in India, but there will be no change to the ceremony. No special arrangements have been made to mark the occasion. This evening at sunset, like every other evening, the clear bugle notes of the Last Post ring out across the sky. Troops of all faiths stop in their tracks and face towards the flagstaff, standing at attention. Those in barracks sitting on their bunks also jump to attention. Slowly, as the notes die away, the Union Jack is lowered. The Englishmen, solemn, salute. Although the ceremony is unchanged and low key, it's different this time and everyone listening knows it. The British flag won't be raised again at this fort on the Frontier. It has also been lowered for the last time in a thousand places across the Jewel in the Crown of the Empire. Slowly the flag is unclipped from its halyard, folded, and handed over to the senior British officer present. He will keep it for a remembrance. It's the end of three centuries of British rule over India. No longer will Ken be known as Lt. Old A.G.E. The need for Assistant Garrison Engineers has come to an end.

Independence Day

April 15, 1947

The next morning dawns full of anticipation. From now on this day will be a national holiday. An Islamic State has come into being. Even Saudi Arabia, home of the Holiest Places, isn't an Islamic State.

Ken waits behind a desk cleared of papers and clean of dust. He has come in early to check that everything is ready for Yusuf to take charge. Ken can hand things over quickly and let Yusuf find his way around what is now his office. They have arranged to meet at nine o'clock.

The wastepaper baskets are empty. The drawers, apart from a few files, are empty. Personal trivia that identified Ken's occupancy has been moved to the Royal Engineers' barracks. The office is as sterile as any new office anywhere. The single file-cover lying inside the top drawer contains nothing more than a welcoming note. No one else is around. Even the office messengers are missing. Mohammed Yusuf comes to the office promptly to the minute. He's wearing his best clothes; it isn't going to be a working day. This day is once in a lifetime. Ken stands up to greet him, and steps aside so Yusuf can sit down. But they remain standing, and hug each other in Punjabi fashion. Ken assures Yusuf, "I'll be available if there are problems." But Yusuf won't want to take advantage of that. Ken congratulates him on his promotion, wishes him well, and shares in his happiness at the formation of his new country and its Independence. Pakistan is on the move and he is its representative. No looking back!

Ken walks down to the main gate of the fort and steps outside.

Any British troops that are still in India are confined to barracks, or fighting fires down on the plains from Peshawar to Calcutta. Lahore is reported to be in flames. There are no units of British troops here. Apart from the few British officers with their Indian troops, there are a couple of enlisted men from the Royal Signals keeping communications open. Ken and two other Royal Engineer officers are responsible for keeping the powerhouse running, the roads open, and the bridges in repair.

The temples are full. The Sikhs are at their *Gurdwara* temple. The civilian Hindus are at their temple, mourning the theft of the great carpet, but knowing it isn't any good fussing about it. Several of the Hindu shopkeepers have decided to open and try to realize some profit from the merchandise they have been unable to dispose of. Others, more cautious, leave the shutters up. There is some fear of the unknown from the Pathans. Those tribesmen are fierce and unpredictable.

The Hindu soldiers have their own small temples in their barracks. The engineers from Southern India also have their own temple. Some, however, choose to not attend and are just writing letters, fearful letters, and wondering whether their letters will actually get sent out or, indeed, whether any of those they have written home in past months have ever gone out. Many, including Ken, haven't had letters from home in months. Home, already far away, suddenly seems much further away.

The Gurkhas have been confined to their barracks. They are unsure how things will turn out back home in Nepal. Their only certainty is that they'll be leaving soon. It will surely mean fighting on the way down to the plains out of these accursed dry brown hills so different from the lush hills of the Khatmandu valley.

All the Muslim men are converging into one of the largest freely assembled gatherings Wana has ever seen. They are congregating in front of, but a good way back from, the tallest flagpole outside the walls of the camp. The men have been gathering since dawn, and have been waiting for a long time. But they aren't impatient. The others inside the walls will still be residents of India, but not these men. At midnight they have lost their Indian nationality forever. Not one has any regrets. There's no sense of anger at the British. Instead, there's nervousness about what's happening all around them and fear that it might prove uncontrollable. There's fear of war with India. There's news filtering through that Lahore is with Pakistan, but that Gurdaspur, the back door to Kashmir, has gone to India. Some of the important Sutlej river works have also gone to India.

The employees of the civil government are also streaming toward the open ground. Villagers are arriving in a steady stream. To the west, where the plain ends against the hills, small white pedestrian figures are moving steadily along the paths that feed into larger ones and then still larger ones as they approach the camp, merging as they come.

The troops, Punjabi Mussulmen, are waiting to move into their lines for customary communal prayer. No dressing to the right or left this time. Standing beside them is the locally recruited militia, a raggle-taggle, but happy mob. Perhaps as many as two thousand Hindu, Sikh, and Gurkha troops still have to make their way down along narrow mountain roads and through a long treacherous river gorge ideal for ambushes. Every full-blooded Muslim promises to himself and to his fellows that these intruders are not going to get out unscathed. Civilian employees inform the Muslim tribesmen and civilians of the preparations of the Hindu troops.

The vast area in front of the flagpole continues to fill with people. Every man is clad in holiday white. The tailors in the camp have been working flat-out for months, making the Indian *shalwar* and *kamize*—white trousers and shirts—for this occasion.

It's breathtakingly memorable. For the first time the flag of Pakistan—a white crescent and star on a green background—

flies proudly from the flagstaff. The brisk breeze supports its pride. The priest holds a microphone and the call to prayer is broadcast through a battery of loudspeakers. The whole ground of white moves in unison, standing, bowing, and kneeling. It's like a great field of grain waving in the wind.

Voices, too, rise and fall like the wind, affirming their faith and new country by repeating over and over: "There is no God but Allah and Mohammed is his prophet. Long live Pakistan!"

The official ceremonies over, Ken makes his way with a few others on the road from Wana to Waziristan and then through the Danasar gorge to Fort Sandeman in Baluchistan. After a rest, it's a long day's journey by truck from there to Quetta. Taking the Bolan Express, they eventually arrive in Karachi. The camp is full of men leaving the Indian sub-continent. Many have wives and children of a different color. Some of these will be leaving. Others will stay. Most of the soldiers will never return.

Like many others, Ken is waiting for the last troopship. It won't come until the latter part of January.

Pakistan

K en wonders what kind of land this is that has newly come into existence as a major state of Islamic faith. It's making the headlines across the world. It has virtually none of the essential material resources that might ensure its viability. The boundary lines dividing Pakistan from India create a country split in two, separated by a thousand miles of potentially hostile territory which is still India. Of the four critical centers of Muslim population, the Bengal delta of the Ganges becomes East Pakistan and the princely state of Hyderabad becomes West Pakistan. One problem with this is that airlines, in times of tension, will have to follow the shipping routes around the toe of India, thus doubling the distance between East and West Pakistan.

Millions of years ago, great natural forces caused the

plates of the earth's surface to slide and buckle. Some rose into great mountains; others sank into great underwater chasms. The screeching distortion separated earth's highest ranges of mountains and peninsula India from central Asia. Eight of the ten highest peaks in the world are to be found in the Karakorums and Himalayas in the north of Pakistan.

Running through these precipitous mountain passes are the rivers that feed Pakistan's growing millions. Primary among them, and eventually receiving its immense flow of water from the others, is the Indus. It begins in Tibet from a spring known as "The Mouth of the Lion." A great earthen dam in the mountains slows its pace as it reaches Kabul. Gated dams are all along its length in order to feed irrigation canals. The last half of its 1,800-mile journey is sluggish except during the monsoons of late summer. Then it becomes a raging lion carrying well over a million cubic feet of water per second away from the drenched and flooded lands of the north. The black clouds roll westwards between the Himalayas. Unable to rise, they swamp not only the Punjab, but Kashmir and all of the Frontier. What has been oppressive heat and dust storms give way to total humidity. Owners of homes with flat roofs discover new holes with every downpour. Delighted little children take off their clothes and dance naked in the rain. Large areas of the Punjab are as flat and wet as the sea that initially created them. They drain slowly and with difficulty.

During the busy decades before the end of British rule, irrigation engineers, using unlimited labor, created the irrigation systems of the Punjab and the Sindh. It is the world's single largest mega irrigation system. Some of the great river-size canals are more than 100 miles long. The desert blossoms. Agricultural communities flourish. Deserts are settled, or resettled. Tiny rivulets from tributaries coming from larger tributaries nourish every field that can be reached and peasants desperately guard their water rights against encroachment or theft.

The fields of wheat, sugar cane, cotton, tobacco, corn, fodder, and fruit trees all flourish. The pattern of life is governed by the monsoons, the winter rains, and the planting times for rice and wheat. Work is hard, but the people have food to eat. An unseen menace is developing, however, which threatens this agricultural success story on which Pakistan is hoping to build its future. The ground water level is rising each year as water is fed onto the land rather than being carried away to the sea. It's bringing to the surface subsoil salts that parch wide areas of the land with white. Eventually Dutch engineers find a solution and the US generosity makes possible an intensive drainage system.

In AD 711, the religion of Pakistan was brought by Mohamed bin Qasim, a 19-year-old general from Basra in Iraq. He defeated the local Hindu rajah at Hyderabad whose forces vastly outnumbered his own. He called a halt to his advance into the Punjab at Multan. Islam is by far the most significant influence on the nation of Pakistan. It's a form of Islam that is zealous and yet broader in tolerance and understanding than some other forms. Its hold over the minds and hearts of the people is unquestionable. It inspires loyalty and devotion and Pakistan's own laws provide for punishment for those who demean it or its Prophet.

For a short while in the 19th century, Sikhism became influential in the north until the British, steadily increasing the areas of India they governed, vanquished the Sikhs and took control of the borders up to Afghanistan.

Plymouth

The final few months of Ken's time in the Army are spent in Egypt, where he's put in charge of a camp for German prisoners-of-war. He is the only one who speaks English. He wishes he had applied himself more carefully to his German studies, but his strict Army officer training stands him in good stead and Captain Old has no problems.

After being discharged in mid-1948, the first job he finds is in Lancashire working as a surveyor on open-cast coal mines. He applies for admission to The Institution of Mechanical Engineers founded in 1847. Tuition is 200 pounds plus an outstanding amount of two pounds, which is presumably from his days at Lincoln. He begins a course in civil engineering in Devonport, a suburb of Plymouth in Devon. This is as close to Cornwall as he can get.

On December 11, 1949, midway through his time in Plymouth, Ken has an encounter with God. His apartment is on Addison Road near the center of Plymouth. He shares a large front bedroom on the second floor with Ken Draper, a bus driver from Barnstaple.

It's about 2.30 a.m. when he is suddenly awake, alertly awake. He listens intently and wonders, 'What woke me up?'

He can hear his friend breathing heavily in sleep in the other bed. He can see the moonlight coming through the window, but his portion of the room is in shadow. Someone, someone unseen, is standing at the right hand side of the bed, two or three feet away. He can't see the visitor; he just knows he's there.

A man's voice speaks in a normal voice, no dialect to notice, but positive and firm in tone. He talks loud enough to hear easily. It's a statement, not a question. "Ken, God has a purpose for your life. He is going to put you to work in a land that is not your own land, among people of a different color and race and culture and creed. He is going to put you to work among boys, and *He* is going to bring it to pass."

His mind races. He believes in God, so it's in His hands to have a purpose for Ken's life, but...

His brother, Joe was a year older. He had been a bomber pilot and was shot down and killed over Yugoslavia just a few days before the end of the war. That leaves Ken as the oldest of the children. He feels a responsibility for his younger siblings. His father and mother are totally stretched in just feeding, clothing, and paying for schooling for their eight children.

Ken is 24 and considers it his duty to make it possible for the family to move into a much larger home. They live on the southeast outskirts of London, and the whole area had been heavily bombed. There was still a great shortage of housing and little prospect for newly married couples to get a place to live. A larger home will mean a married couple can stay at home until they find a place of their own.

The voice continues speaking for about a quarter of an hour before Ken gives his answer. "Give me three years first and God can have the rest of my life." He says it, he means it, and never swerves from it.

Over the three years that Ken is in Plymouth, he maintains a strict routine that includes a rather unique ritual. Every morning, rain or shine, summer and winter, he walks over to Plymouth Hoe and down the steps to the road below. From the road, a narrow path leads down to the rocky outcroppings around the Sound. One rock in particular, about 14 feet above the water, has a flat top. Removing his outer clothes to reveal a swimsuit, Ken dives into the icy water and swims out to the buoy in the harbor and back. In winter the water is so cold it's like being hit over the head with a brick. No one else is foolish enough to swim in the Sound in the wintertime, but Ken stays healthy year around and never catches a cold.

Back to Pakistan

When Ken graduates with his degree in civil engineering, he works for a year in Southend, Essex at the headland of the Thames River. He later finds employment with the Borough of Engineers. In August, 1952, Ken buys a house twice the size of the one in Days Lane. His parents and siblings move the few miles from there to Wheathill Road, Anerley. Five marriages take place there and the young couples live at home until they can find places of their own.

It's nearly three years since Ken made his bargain with God. The time has almost ticked away. What can he expect to happen now?

The Thames flooding in January 1953 has every available engineer in the Borough engaged in draining the islands and repairing the breaches in the sea walls with sandbags. Once the walls are raised above tide levels, attention is turned further towards London. Repairs are urgently needed on the river wall just upstream of the projected tunnel crossing of the Thames at Dartford. It's here that Ken, as a Resident Engineer, discovers by accident what is going to happen next.

It is now five months past the deadline he gave God for letting Him have the rest of his life. Picking up a newspaper, never available in his previous job, it seems to fall open by itself to the third page from the back. Shining out from the many columns of small print as though it is printed in red, is an advertisement for a civil engineer in Pakistan. He stares at it a long time. It stirs many pleasant memories of the time spent in that area which was once India. It is, of course, no coincidence that Ken's eyes focus so immediately on that particular advertisement! Although Ken isn't aware of it just yet, God is beginning to move him toward the ultimate plans He has for his life. In case Ken has need for confirmation, God arranges for Geoff, Ken's brother, to mail him the exact same advertisement. Ken takes the hint and mails off his application.

Things move quickly, and by the middle of July Ken is being introduced to his future employers in Karachi at the southern end of Pakistan. He's told straight away, "You aren't being employed for your engineering ability, but for your integrity. That's why you're receiving such a high salary. You will be going to Wah in the north to build a new ordnance factory. It will make military weapons and ammunition." Ken takes a plane to Rawalpindi. He decides that a car won't be either safe or reliable, and buys himself an old Norton commando motorcycle instead. Besides, he has always wanted one and now is his opportunity.

Accustomed to attending church at least once every Sunday

since his childhood, Ken quickly finds a Sunday evening service at the nearby mission hospital. Most of those who attend are American missionaries, but they gladly welcome this maverick engineer from England.

It is early spring 1954. The road from Wah to Rawalpindi is about 23 miles. The narrow, two-lane rutted road has dirt shoulders. It's the main road for traffic from Karachi in the far south going through Lahore up to Peshawar and on to the North West Frontier. There are scores of trucks taking quarried limestone from the Margalla and Wah hills to the plains of the Punjab and beyond. In summer, lines of bullock carts heaped with cauliflowers for the Rawalpindi market, add to the congestion.

Ken can normally expect to make it from Wah to Rawalpindi in about 21 minutes on his motorcycle. On this particular journey he isn't traveling by motorcycle, but by car. He has to follow behind a slow moving truck over-laden with stone. Once through the pass on the Rawalpindi side, he pulls out to pass it. The road is clear of traffic. The truck, now heading downhill, is speeding up rapidly. Midway through passing it, the car develops a steering wobble. Ken can't control the wobble, and because the brakes are bad, he can't slacken speed. The car, with Ken still in it, careens down the side of the hill, flipping over and over as it goes. The truck hasn't stopped.

When the car comes to a standstill, Ken checks himself for damage. No broken bones, a bump or two on his head, a bit of blood here and there, but nothing serious. He searches for his glasses, but can't find them. This is disturbing because he is very near-sighted. The car, even for Pakistan, is a complete write-off. It's nothing short of a miracle that he's escaped, for the road is 60 to 100 feet above him. The car has landed plumb in the middle of a small, level, scrub-covered area only about 15 feet below the road level. A few feet on either side and Ken would not have survived.

As he makes his way slowly back up to the road, he's thinking about his narrow escape...and praying. "Thank you, God, for saving my life. I acknowledge afresh the promise I made to You.

Since I should be dead, You have every right to the rest of my life and You can have it."

He flags down a bus which takes him to Sarai Kala. Then he takes a tonga up to the hospital. Dr. Brown is a friend and they occasionally play chess together. Ken asks him, "Will you just check me over? I've been in a car accident." After he does, he suggests, "You need to rest for a while. You can use our guest bedroom."

Up until now the day had gone relatively smoothly. When Ken wakes up, he decides to make his way home. He can't find Dr. Brown to thank him, and decides he'll just write him a note later. As he goes out through the main gate, about to get into a tonga, something akin to the Damascus Road Experience occurs. A seven or eight-foot-tall— more like nine-foot-tall— avenging angel clad in shining white like a nurse's uniform, has swords of the Apocalypse in both hands. She lashes out in a tongue that feels like machine gun bullets manufactured in New England and every one a hit, "WHERE DO YOU THINK YOU'RE GOING?"

Let's pause here, and recognize his independence of action. He hasn't been admitted to the hospital, no paperwork has been done, and he has every right to go home. However, his tremulous explanation brings the incisive response "GET BACK INTO THAT BED!" Not even a please!

Ever since then he allows women the last word and especially Dorothy Christy.

Wah Cottage

The District Engineer from Karachi and his wife have just returned north. They are English and invite Ken to come out and visit them at the cottage where they are staying. Nestling against the hill-slope beside a bridge is a little white dream cottage with a beautiful miniature garden planted with a wide variety of colorful flowers. Beyond is the Grand Trunk Road. Little rivulets of crystal water coming from springs higher up wander in and out past the flower beds. Eventually the water spills into the river. There's even a diversion to bring water into a swimming pool hidden by a hedge from anyone on the bridge above. Guests drinking tea on the porch can watch close up the fascinating traffic on the east-west artery of India in its endless variety—military vehicles, cars, lines of camels, oxcarts, donkey carts, herds of goats, flocks of sheep, brightly colored buses, trucks, bicycles, and pedestrians.

Ken immediately falls in love with the place. He's shown many kindnesses. They let him know he is always welcome and he visits frequently. The enduring heritage that the English have left all over the world from its rapidly disappearing colonial empire, isn't monuments, great buildings, institutions, or forms of government, but, quite simply, the domestic gardens that homesick wives have created. They have, with the patient instinct of rural England, harmonized the voluptuous beauty, rapid growth, and often exceptional size and color of new plants using trusted favorites from home. These are not native to temperate zones. Many of these gardens will surely remain long after all the English are gone.

Always curious, Ken wants to know more of the history of Wah Cottage. It was originally known as Gammon Cottage. It's necessary to go back to when Pakistan becomes a country of its own. There is little hope of economic survival. It has no industry and very limited road infrastructure to support commerce and movement of goods. There is a small cement factory in Karachi, another in Sindh at Rohri and, to provide for the needs of the entire Punjab and Frontier Province, a cement factory at Wah. Pakistan's strategic lifeline is the road from Karachi northeast to Lahore and then northwest to Peshawar up to the Khyber Pass. A bridge crosses the Dhamra River just after the turn on the left to Wah village. Beyond the Dhamra to the right is the road to the cement factory. Should the bridge be out of commission, then the link to the Frontier will be broken and the supplies of cement by road to the whole of the Punjab would be in jeopardy.

The narrow, single-track bridge is built of limestone arches. It has never been designed for the wheeled traffic that is now using it. The need for replacement is urgent. The contract for the construction of the new reinforced concrete bridge is given to an engineering company established in India by a British engineer, John Gammon. The company has to do well on this contract. It's one of their first in Pakistan.

The great limestone hill that is being quarried belongs to the Hayat family of Wah village. They have moved from the ancestral home there and built a glorious new mansion overlooking the Dhamra River on a spur across the Grand Trunk Road. Across the river to the right are the chimneys of the cement factory.

The chief engineer needs to live on-site to oversee the bridge construction. Almost underneath the bridge itself, he negotiates a site for the cottage he will build. This particular site is owned by Mahmud Hayat Khan, a resident of Lahore. He has a sister named Bilquis. The site is steep, but the house can be built against the hill, and the garage, on the upper floor, can have access from the lane going to Wah village. The cottage will be rent-free, eventually reverting to the owner of the land.

In researching the history of the cottage, Ken discovers another interesting bit of information about this location. A legend, dating from the early 16th-century, claims that one day the founder of the Sikhs, Guru Nanak, was sitting by the springs at the foot of the hill. His Muslim rival, living on the top of the hill, pushed a great stone down towards the guru. Gathering momentum as it fell, other stones and pebbles followed in its wake. The guru turned towards the thundering noise and, about to be crushed in the avalanche, put up his hand to protect himself. Such were his miraculous powers that the stone stopped rolling and provided protection until all the smaller stones rattled past and the noise and the dust subsided. Imprinted in the stone, clear and deeply embedded, is a full-size, perfect hand-print— the hand-print of Guru Nanak. Every year in April, many Sikhs travel to one of their holiest places, the Holy Hand-print. Although it's no longer part of India, the pilgrims are invariably treated with courtesy and welcomed as guests.

Ken has no idea that one day he himself will be privileged to live in the cottage. By that time, it will have been renamed 'Peniel' by Bilquis Sheikh.

South to the Desert

K en enjoys his time in Wah. The work is satisfying and he meets many fine people on Sunday evenings. His theology doesn't always square with theirs, but he allows that they have as much right to their opinions as he does to his.

He's been at the ordnance factory for just nine months when he's instructed to hand over the work to his Pakistani assistant and get down to Hyderabad as quickly as possible. A cement factory is being built several miles outside the city on the Badin road and the construction has run into problems.

At the end of April, Ken and three workmen drive south through the Thal desert to Hyderabad. The drive will be challenging as it is about 800 miles away, and the most direct route naturally has the worst roads. The spare tire is as bare of tread as the other four and it's virtually impossible to buy any replacements. Ken intends to go non-stop if possible. He will do all the driving himself. However, if necessary, the carpenter could drive short distances.

Making use of the full moon, they leave before dawn to get as many hours of cool driving in as possible. The stony, barren roads across the Salt Range plateau give way to tracks that are little more than bundled straw strewn on sand to make a roadbed.

The hot season is close to its peak and they carefully ration their drinking water. Tea shops are only available at the infrequent road junctions.

After a long day, they are once again driving in the moonlight. Ken, tired before he left, drops off at the wheel. He wakes and sees a right-angled bend suddenly in front of him. With only seconds to spare, he wrenches the wheel violently to steer the car around it. Prudently, he pulls over to rest until dawn.

Late the next morning, the car breaks down. After taking them 550 miles of their journey, the engine has overheated. Promising to be back, Ken hitches a ride on a desert truck to a cement factory not too distant. The British manager, realizing Ken is suffering from heat stroke, immediately puts him to bed in a darkened, air-conditioned room. What lovely bliss! Ken wakes up in the evening to find the car has arrived at the factory under its own steam. It has been repaired, and the three passengers are waiting for him to continue driving through the night.

There have been three places in the world that Ken felt he would never want to live. The first is Wigan, a coal and mill town in Lancashire, England. When he was returning to his Army base from a visit in Cornwall, he caught glimpses from the train of wet, dirty tar-blackened roofs gripped by fog. Mile after mile of utterly depressing scenery. And what would be his first assignment as a surveyor after the Army? Of course—Wigan, where he discovers the golden hearts of Lancashire people.

A second place is Port Said at the northern end of the Suez Canal. On a brief break from the troopship carrying him to India, he and his fellow travelers had marched briskly around the town for exercise. Some, who bought drinks from the vendors running alongside, went temporarily blind from wood alcohol poisoning. It seemed to be a sinkhole of iniquity. A little more than a year later, he found himself working with a detachment of German prisoners of war across the canal from Port Said.

The third place is Hyderabad in the Sindh Desert. It is very different from either the Frontier or the Potwar plateau of the Punjab where he worked before. He first went through it by rail a couple of months after leaving Wazeristan. It's a mono-color city—dirt brown. Its great fort on the hill is mud-walled. Its houses are mud-walled. Hyderabad has the greatest density of fly population ever encountered. It's crowded with refugees from India who live in shacks along the railroad tracks. Now Ken decides being sent to Hyderabad is putting God's humor to the test. Ever after that he holds his peace about places he doesn't want to work.

Ken is the civil engineering contractor's agent on the site. Initially he's the only foreigner working at the cement factory site other than the Dane who is supervising the general construction. His employers have several hundred workers already in place, brought in from other jobs, but the start-up is in trouble.

The site is a few miles to the south of Hyderabad, a town in one of the hottest deserts in the world, the Thar Desert. It's only a few miles from the Indus River, which, after its long journey from Tibet, now approaches the sea. Good quantities of both gypsum and limestone are available. The project is being jointly financed by the governments of New Zealand and Pakistan and its name thus becomes the Zeal-Pak cement factory.

Ken and Marie

Ken first meets Marie in February, 1954, at the Frontier Conference for missionaries held at Taxila Hospital. He isn't a missionary, but attends Bible Study there on Sunday nights. Marie, a widow, works as a missionary nurse at the hospital. In April Ken is transferred to Hyderabad, thus missing any opportunity to get better acquainted with her.

However, in November he receives a letter from her letting him know that she will be arriving in early December. She will be with a team of literacy experts under the leadership of Dr. Laubach. Marie is *so* glad to see him! If she hadn't been a missionary, she might even have kissed him!

A major problem develops when their hotel reservations are cancelled by the government. Ken quickly arranges for the team to stay with him. The team leaves just before Christmas, but Marie and a friend stay for the holiday. They have pretty well exhausted subjects of conversation. They usually spend any free evening silently listening to classical music and just enjoying each other's company.

Marie returns to Taxila and Ken continues his work on the cement factory project. He is now receiving additional help from other expatriates. Workmen at the site suffer multiple injuries, and Ken writes to Marie frequently asking for medical advice.

Winter warms into spring and on to an unbearably hot summer. Little of the refreshing monsoon rains reaches as far as Hyderabad.

In September Ken receives notice he's to move up to Karachi to work on a Dry Dock. He is happy to be moving further north. He's due some leave before he begins this next assignment and decides to spend the time in Taxila. He'll stay with the Browns. Surprisingly, it is Marie who meets him at the station. She has returned from a summer in Murree and is now being transferred to Sialkot. Before she has to leave, she and Ken spend the days together. Ken is thinking he would like to ask Marie to be his wife, but having given his life to God, he isn't sure if marriage is in God's plan for him.

He kneels and talks to God about the strange thing that's happening to him. He wants to get it right. "God, I don't know what's happening. All I know is that I have promised You can have the rest of my life. I meant that then, and I mean it still. The rest of my life is Yours. If it fits within Your will for me to ask Marie to marry me, I want You to stop the car tonight just in front of the shisham tree that's 30 yards short of Gilani's garage so that I'll know. I need to know for sure, God. Amen."

Marie is driving and they are making good time. Suddenly, she pulls to the side of the road directly in front of the shisham tree. "I think there's something wrong with the tire." Ken smiles. He knows there's nothing wrong with the tire. God has answered his prayer. But he gets out to look. When he gets back in the car, he says, "Marie, will you marry me?" She doesn't answer so he repeats the question, "I'm asking you to marry me." She smiles and asks, "Isn't there someone you should ask first?" "No, I'm of age and know my mind." She nods and says, "Yes!" And they kiss for the first time.

Shortly after Ken and Marie are married God moves them to an orphanage. This becomes part of the training Ken needs before God can use him where intended. Over and over again, Ken experiences the subtle way God works to strengthen his faith. The faithfulness and provision of God, His perfect timing, and the way He uses people to complete His purposes are constant reminders of what a great God we have.

Ken and Marie will soon be replaced at the orphanage and will be returning to Sialkot. In June of 1957, the personnel committee of the Sialkot Mission appoints them as missionaries for a term of three years. Ken, although he isn't a trained missionary, has never planned to be a missionary, and doesn't consider himself to be a missionary, instantly becomes one.

In September 1957 it's time to leave the orphanage. Ken had promised Dr. Orval Hamm that he would convert a disused TB ward at the hospital into a children's ward. He'll begin work on that as soon as he and Marie return from England where they plan to adopt a baby. That becomes more complicated than they imagined. A certificate of marriage is required. This would be no problem except that the marriage certificate was eaten by white ants. It's necessary to obtain an affidavit of marriage from the minister who performed the ceremony.

> I, William Sutherland, ordained minister of the Gospel, belonging to the United Presbyterian Church in the United States of America and having a license and authority to perform marriages in Great Britain, India, Pakistan, and the United States of America, do hereby declare that I performed the marriage between

Kenneth G. Old, son of W. R. Old,
British Citizen, Bachelor, born in Cornwall
on the second day of May 1925

and

Marie McGuill, widow, daughter of
S. Johnson, citizen of the United States of
America, born in Butte, Montana, USA.
on the 28th day of July 1914.

That the marriage took place in the American Mission Hospital at Taxila, West Pakistan on the 29th day of December 1955.

Witnesses to the marriage and signed on their marriage certificate were

Dorothy Christy
Stuart Cowbourne

William Sutherland

The child they adopt is a boy they name Timothy, who naturally brings massive changes, but also great blessings into their lives.

Marie spends most of her time being housewife and mother to Timothy. She often wonders, 'Where does he get all his energy?' He's now two and bursting with growth. He makes his clamorous needs known in three languages—Urdu, Punjabi, and English—in the order of fluency and they often have to have his Punjabi interpreted for them as neither of them is as fluent in that language as he is. His bedtime stories, in contrast to space age stories, feature water buffaloes, camels, bullock carts, and lately, steam rollers and tar boilers as he sees road repairs being done.

Timothy goes with Ken to buy bricks. He experiences six new 'firsts.'

1) Saw a train!
2) Saw an airplane!!
3) Sat in the seat of a tractor for over an hour!

4) Ate boiled eggs and drank tea in a country village.

5) Saw a dead snake killed in the garden.

6) Played with some tiddlers in the garden pond.

He went to bed tired and happy.

It's while working on the project for Orval that Ken meets with disaster. He's up on the roof. Unbeknownst to him, a laborer moves the ladder to use in another place. Ken begins to back down off the roof. Instead of landing on a firm step, his foot finds empty space. He lands on the ground in a sitting position, damaging several discs in his spine. The workmen hurry over to help him up. Ken stops them from moving him, and tells them, "Go find a doctor immediately." Surgery is recommended, but Ken refuses to have any operation. He chooses instead to live with the subsequent pain, and suffers from it throughout the remainder of his life. And it puts an end to his motorcycle riding.

When Ken completes the conversion of the children's ward, he's sent to Murree to work on much needed student housing for Junior and Senior High school students at the missionary school. The Sandes Home, a former rest home for British soldiers, requires extensive reconstruction to be suitable for use as a boarding house. The weather halts work and he returns to Sialkot for the winter. He and Marie are delighted to be informed that the mission has given them permission to rent accommodation away from the hospital. They are aware that Gammon Cottage, on the other side of Wah Cantonment, in Wah village is empty. They contact Mahmud Hayat Khan, who agrees to let them rent it. The two winters they spend there are times of great personal happiness.

Ken had expected to start building a church in the residential area of the huge new ordnance factory. For six years the small Christian community has been contributing to a fund to provide a place of worship. However, in the three months Ken was down from Murree, he is only able to get an eye ward started at the nearby Mission Hospital in Taxila.

He returns to Murree in March to complete work there and goes back to Wah in August. The building of the church is now under way. The ground breaking ceremony is held on October 27 with many Pakistani and English folks present. The church could be finished in four or five months if building materials are available. Prospects aren't too good though. After seven months of almost weekly visits to Rawalpindi endeavoring to obtain cement, Ken begins work with only 50 of the approximately 900 bags of cement he will need. He began in faith, expecting the Lord will provide the necessary supplies as needed. Since then he receives 200 more bags in these days. That is truly a miracle. He keeps praying for the other 650 bags. Many other things including bricks, nails, screws, and glass are in short supply and difficult to find. But he goes on in faith with what he has. Recently the good news came that a church at home is undertaking to help with the cost of the building.

Besides this building work, Ken has been taking a Sunday evening service and a weekly Bible class for the British folks in the factory. He and Marie have also been entertaining a number of these folks in their home.

Recently he's been taking the train to a town nearly 200 miles away. The staff quarters being built at a Mission Hospital there are now almost finished.

Ken and Marie anticipate a joyful Christmas. Timothy will have a wonderful time exploring a stocking full of surprises. There will be a church service on the new church site where a garage is serving as the church building. There will be a service for the European community in the factory. They will probably have dinner with the Pakistani staff of the Taxila Hospital. There will be carol singing, good fellowship, thoughts of home, and far off friends. They will all be sharing in the recollection of that first Christmas day, and God's great gift of a Savior.

Return from Furlough

Ken and Marie devote the first six months of their furlough in 1961 fulfilling obligations to report to the churches in the States on the work being done in Pakistan. Congregations in New York, Illinois, Tennessee, Kansas, Colorado, Idaho, Washington, and Alaska benefit from Ken's insightful and enthusiastic preaching.

In Washington, Ken spends a week at Camp Ghormley and another at Tall Timber Ranch ministering to young boys at summer camp. They fall in love with him and hang on his every word. He also leads a Sunday School class.

After they leave Washington in the fall, they make their way to New York in the little red car and then by sea to England. The final six months are spent in England. Timmy never tires of visiting the Tower of London to see the Queen's jewels.

Ken and Marie need to complete the adoption of Timmy. They also want to adopt another child. Colin is a ginger-haired little boy some four months older than Timmy. In March the process of adopting both boys is complete. They are very close friends, and they play with each other and fight each other in about equal measure.

At the end of May, they all arrive in Karachi. Almost as soon as they land, they receive an invitation to a welcoming party at the Orphanage. Over 50 of the 70 girls are away on holiday visiting a relative, but 17 have no relatives at all, so it is especially pleasant that Mama and Poppa visit.

The children, most of them barefooted, cluster around with all the news—Mary has a beautiful baby; crippled old Babboo is still saving hard from her five cents a week pocket money. Lily, eyes twinkling, catches Ken's hand and clutches it tight. Sweet Hassin smiles happily, and Zarin dances traditional Punjabi dances of welcome as she traces delicate pictures with her hands. Carefully rehearsed songs of welcome follow a meal of curried patties and sweet, fried candies. During their stay in Washington, a kind neighbor had given them cloth for dresses for the girls. How their eyes pop at the sight of that material and how delighted they are with a couple of pencils each. Later, as they sing 'Count Your Many Blessings' in Urdu, it humbles Ken to see how completely they mean what they sing where their only certainty is that God *will* provide for them. Ken's Pakistani friend, who is responsible for looking after the accounts of the Orphanage, confides "It's most wonderful. As you know we rely on prayer to sustain us. Not once have we been in debt. Usually we have no more than $100 in our purse and frequently less than half that. It costs $350 a month to feed the 70 children. Often taxes exceed $100 at one blow, and yet—God always provides. He is always faithful."

While Ken and Marie lived at the Orphanage, they too found this wonderful faithfulness of God to those who love and trust Him.

Marie is a supervisor at the language school where Ken is taking classes with other missionaries. They study the languages of the various areas where they'll be working. The students have come from varied and distant places—USA (Oregon), Korea, Denmark, Sweden, Finland, New Zealand, Australia, and the UK. Tim and Colin attend the school for mission kids which was started in an empty church in 1954. Now it is bursting at the seams with an enrollment of 160. The rickety bus they ride to school careens around hairpin bends on the narrow, mountain road.

Ken has to register his car and finds this is a much different procedure than in the States. At the first office, the official gives him three or four forms and directs him to the police station. The superintendent there is busily involved in filling out a charge sheet against a subordinate who had accepted an application for a religious procession from a man who had died, so he could not possibly have signed it. This unhappy subordinate is also charged with allowing one of the men involved in nine murders to escape.

Ken becomes involved in a warm discussion on the chances of the Pakistani cricket team now touring in England. Ken is more optimistic about the success of the Pakistani team than the superintendent, and the various forms are soon signed. All that remains now is paying the fee.

This proves a major undertaking. The stamps for this purpose are only sold by a cripple whose office is a small, wooden cage about 6' x 3' x 5' high. It's continually surrounded by 30 to 50 Punjabis trying to buy stamps. While hands clutching rupees and scribbled notes reach through the slats in the cage, the air is filled with the sounds of constant clamoring for attention to be next. Each purchase requires an entry in the ledger, and the clerk sits on the floor recording names of those fortunate enough to obtain stamps in a huge register. Four others are also crowded into the cage—three wanting to buy court stamps and a man selling sheets of judicial paper.

Having made no progress after a quarter of an hour in the jostling crowd, Ken decides to work his way around to the door of the cage. 20 minutes later, perspiring profusely, he finally manages to get up to the door opening itself, not really sure whether this is actually the booth that sells the tax stamps.

Another ten minutes and a space inside the cage becomes available and a cordial invitation is extended. The cage is unbearably hot with its tin roof, but at least it is more relaxing, if that adjective might be used in this situation.

Ken, as he signs his name, notices that others have applied their thumbprints in lieu of signatures. Once the tax stamps are affixed, Ken grasps his papers with a sigh of relief. The clerk closes his ledger and disappointed purchasers turn away; they will return early tomorrow to try again.

When Ken arrives back at the first office, it's also closing and he's informed, "You must come back tomorrow." That isn't possible, he's leaving town tonight. He hopes he isn't asked for his registration certificate until he can manage to get back to obtain one.

Although Ken has grown accustomed to the intense heat of Pakistan, he finds the journey from Karachi up to Murree most uncomfortable. Because the temperatures range between 115 and 120 degrees in the shade, Marie and the boys go by plane. Ken intends to travel the 1,000 miles by car, but the vehicle doesn't behave itself. Ultimately, it's left in a garage with the engine grumbling, 'I was never meant to be used in such heat.' Once rested, recovered, and repaired, the car grudgingly travels the final miles to Murree.

New Home in Sialkot

In September, the Mission assigns Ken the task of taking over the operation of a boys' boarding school in Sialkot. CTI is the Christian Training Institute. It's in the very center of a Christian area and provides education to village boys, almost all Christian. The school often has short-term younger teachers from the States with an interest in athletics. Some of Pakistan's best athletes and basketball players have come from CTI.

Their house has over 30 rooms. The missionary couple who

lived here for 40 years has retired. Now Ken and Marie are responsible for running it and looking after it. One Sunday Ken left church early with the boys and tried to get in the house. In doing so, he counted 21 outside doors, but all were so well locked up he couldn't get in! Almost immediately after arriving, Marie finds herself with a houseful of guests. The huge annual convention of missionaries brings Christians from all over Pakistan. The very large tent on the school grounds seats something like a thousand people. The convention lasts a week. Many of the speakers are foreigners and they stay with Ken and Marie, but they only sleep there and eat their meals with the convention. They can have up to eleven guests. Many Pakistani speakers stay in other places on the compound. There are hundreds and hundreds and hundreds of people sleeping in tents out in the open at night. It's a wonderful thing to see. Ken and Marie take turns going to the meeting so that one of them is home with the boys.

Many of the rooms are very large. Ken remarked in a startled voice, "Do you know that Audrey's whole house, both upstairs and downstairs, could fit into our bedroom with a third of the space still left? And Jean's house could also easily fit into our bedroom." It sounds impossible that a room could be that size and that high, but it is, and the sitting room is even bigger. Ken has had about 70 Pakistani boys in that room on a Sunday evening for the Christian Endeavour meeting. There could easily have been more.

They take one section for their 'sort of' private apartment. It has two huge bedrooms—each with its own bathroom—and then small rooms, one of which is a private sitting room and one a quiet study for Ken. There's another bathroom off the study. Then in another part of the house Ken has his office. Across from the big sitting room is a three-room apartment where the Brazils live. He's a retired bank manager from Lloyd's in England, and she's a lecturer at the Church of Scotland in Sialkot. The two couples have all their meals together in the very large dining room. Although the house looks elegant, there's no hot water and no bath tubs. The roof is mud and leaks.

Marie's duties start with morning tea for all of them at 6 a.m. Breakfast is at 7:00. Then she attends to all the duties of the house—order the meals, go over the accounts with the cook, see that the cleaning gets done, have morning worship with the servants. Just now there are five of them because the whole house is in use and has to be kept clean. One is temporary and will be leaving after the convention is over. The necessity for so much help is because all the floors have to be cleaned every single day. 30 are a lot of rooms to be cleaned. There are always guests and there's a huge garden—literally acres of it—to keep up. About 8:15 Marie takes the boys to school and then goes to the hospital where she works in the operating room until noon. The boys have to be picked up at 1:15. After lunch they rest and Marie does all of the leftover chores. Life isn't one bit dull. But they are happy to be back and feel useful again. They will both be very busy, but they love it and enjoy wonderful fellowship with others. All the missionaries are one large family no matter what country they come from. There's a deep love and concern that Marie has never seen anywhere else.

Ken has to wait until the convention is over to get started on his building work. His first job is to finish an extension of the school chapel that he started before they went to England.

Summer Volunteers

For we are His workmanship, created in Christ Jesus
for good works which God prepared beforehand
that we should walk in them.
Ephesians 2:10

Duane, a young Peace Corps agriculturist, is so mad he could hardly eat his supper of boiled beans in the village that night. He was convinced that if he could persuade the local peasant farmers to plant their rice seedlings in rows it would facilitate weeding and enhance crops. But the local farmers don't see it that way at all. Why, even when Raja Sulwan was Lord of Sialkot they were planting their seedlings at random and had managed alright. Besides, how are they going to weed the rice anyway?

Duane is ready for this one. He has brought a sample weed eater from East Pakistan. Since the Pakistani co-worker isn't there to interpret, he tries to demonstrate, but the planting is too thin. This amuses the watchers. Duane, madder than ever under the hot sticky sun, runs it through the nursery patch of seedlings and convinces them in about five seconds flat. It isn't enough, however, to persuade them to plant their seedlings in rows. They leave and go share the hookah under the peepul tree. Duane's fire is up. Several women are cajoled into coming and plant. He stretches his solitary line out straight, and the women start planting along it—until the men come over and abuse the women for being foolish. Next, a group of men from another area are persuaded and their example arouses the group of squatting men to come and plant too. Now there isn't enough line for all of them, so they crowd together planting on the one line. The quick abuse the slow, and Duane dreams of spending Sundays back in Minnesota.

This is a parable too. A parable of Christian life—the guiding and setting of lives in straight lines, in an ordered way, bringing out the value of a God directed life. It also emphasizes the need of persistence through discouragement. One of the younger missionaries doesn't return after her first term. She tells of the shock she felt in being 'unwanted.' She found little desire, even in the Christian community, for a new kind of 'Christian planting.' For them, new experiences, no matter how valuable, can't replace inheritance. Ken finds that one of the most essential characteristics of the Christian life is this quality of perseverance, continuing to push against brick walls whether they yield or not. Unpleasant duties must be seen as Christian responsibilities to be completed rather than left at the first hurdle.

For all their reluctance to accept Duane's ideas, the rice farmers are seeing an agricultural revolution taking place. Several years ago tractors were only hauling city refuse. Now, more and more are replacing the pair of oxen and the wooden plow in plowing, harrowing, and rolling seedlings into the ground. Nearby, the Persian wheel has given way to the diesel driven pump. The owners of this gushing water supply planted their rice weeks before those waiting for the monsoon rains.

Audrey Campbell, a pretty girl from Pennsylvania, has found her corner in a leper colony in Rawalpindi. Many of the lepers come from Kashmir. Doctors come in weekly from Taxila Hospital to advise treatment, but otherwise Audrey is alone. She tries to keep the untainted children in a separate portion of the compound away from their infected parents. Although she provides activities for rehabilitation of the elders, they often prefer to sneak away begging in the bazaars. There are many other missionaries in nursing 'corners' here and she feels privileged to work among such dedicated people.

The weaver birds build their nests high this year. During late June the colony of yellow-breasted cocks select a palm tree not far away. There is loud flutter and chatter as they set to work! As soon as the nests are complete, a bevy of bright little hens come to choose their new home and the builder becomes their mate. The tradition goes that when weaver birds build high it's because they know a flood is coming and past disastrous floods are quoted authoritatively.

The town courthouse has a large sign, 'Flood Control Center' and a ten-foot high levee has been bulldozed. The hospital staff houses are prepared—furniture is perched on brackets and bricks a foot or so above the floor. There's light flooding in some of the agricultural areas on the other side of the city. The river is within a foot of the top of the banks and looks likely to overflow if there is further rain. Up until now, the monsoon has been light and considerate. It started late and has rarely rained for more than two hours. So the land is green, the dust settled, and hardly a day's building work has been lost.

At the hospital the building of a new bungalow (with a floor well above the previous five-foot flood level) is progressing well. Western ideas and methods of construction have brought visits from curious city engineers. In Pasrur, 30 miles to the east, the school building is up to roof level and its verandahs are being prepared for use as classrooms when the school reopens on Monday (floods permitting). In Gujranwala, 30 miles to the southwest, the hostel for 130 boys is claiming more and more attention. The boys will attend the Christian Technical Training School and will be learning technical trades such as carpentry, blacksmithing, tailoring, and shoemaking.

Marie is now counting the days until the end of school, but the three months in the summer for the boys' schooling are a necessary separation. The boys also want to be back home in Sialkot with their tree-house and many Pakistani friends. She and the boys don't expect to see Ken hardly at all this summer apart from a snatched weekend or two. But he gets called up to Murree to help with problems at the new school hostel for missionary kids. The hillside at the end of the building has been eroded by rain, and is slipping away. A retaining wall has to be built in a hurry.

Returning to Sialkot, Ken and Marie welcome Ed and Audrey Carlson from the States into their house. They will be studying language hard all winter under Marie's supervision.

The boys from Murray College put on a whole evening of skits, complete with music, with hardly any outside help. It was well attended, and Ken is richly encouraged by the attention these boys always give to the closing devotions. It's a fine opportunity to show that their faith is more a list of 'Do's' rather than 'Do not's'. Ken has to miss a retreat which he is supposed to direct because he's called back to Murree. This new venture of following-up the summer hill camps with retreats in the plains is a fruitful extension of work among the young people.

There is considerable need for additional dedicated young people willing to spend their lives way off in a corner for Christ's sake. Ken writes to church congregations in America asking them to remember the responsibility Christians have to be an example and portray Him who first loved us in any work they do. Too many these days stand aside rather than become involved in problems they prefer not to make their own. The Christian cannot stand aside if his duty points clearly to becoming involved... and everyone can become involved in prayer.

Murree

Murree, at an altitude of 7,400 feet, is on a ridge in the foothills of the Himalayan Mountains. It was founded as a hill station by the British in 1851 and many who came stayed on, settling in and raising families. Even in the summer it cools down in the evening, and actually gets chilly. Murree has become the summer retreat for the governor of the Punjab—allowing escape from the heat of the plains, which is so oppressive from late May to early September.

The Murree Christian School was built in 1956 to educate the children of missionaries. It offers high quality Christian education in a Christian atmosphere.

Staff, as well as the students, come from around the world. Tim and Colin are sent off to this boarding school in 1963. It's difficult to know who is more stressed, the children or the parents. A note addressed to 'Dear Daddy Old' arrives.

Dear Daddy

> I want you.
> I am homesik for you.
> Come up to Murree as fast as you can.
> I have a sore leg Daddy.
>
> Love Tim Bimbo

What a heart-wrenching note to receive. Ken, of course, does not, cannot, go rescue his youngest son. The times during school breaks are extra sweet.

Murree spreads along the top of a ridge for about three miles. The resorts along the ridge provide respite and wonderful views of pine forests amidst magnificent mountain scenery. One sizzling hot summer on the plains finds Ken and Marie in one of these resorts. They have the same room they had before in the rambling building owned by the mission. The building is surrounded by a forest of fir, pine, oak, and Christmas wreath holly. The wind from the north whirls the rain against the windows of the chalet like bullets and wails like a banshee through the tops of the tall firs. The neighboring peaks are blotted out by scraps of clouds blown up over the ridge from the valley below. The cold wind is a welcome relief from the heat of the plains though. Taxila and Rawalpindi led the whole country with 118 degrees in the shade before they left and that was hot enough for anyone. They are enjoying the mountain air, the scenery, and the fellowship of other missionaries.

Marie is jack-knifed against the head of the bed, a blanket around her legs, knitting like mad to complete a coat sweater of very intricate design. Her other sweater just gave out at the elbows, giving added incentive for finishing this one in a hurry. She has become quite a knitter in her infrequent spare moments having made two for Ken and this is the second for herself. Ken can wear his in broad daylight, too.

This is an attractive mountain retreat. In this land of over 48 million population, and constantly prying eyes, it has that rare commodity—privacy. Privacy shared by five families which includes 16 adults and five children. But there is privacy from outsiders. Except for their steep, twisting, and muddy driveway, the roads are all paved and there is even a bus service of sorts. The hilly city of Murree is two miles away on a slightly higher ridge. They can walk over there for church on Sundays, for infrequent shopping expeditions, and for an occasional committee meeting. The church services are a special treat because they're in English. This is a joy after the Urdu and Punjabi services throughout the rest of the year on the plains. There is a choir as well, which Ken leads on occasion. The adult Bible class has always been a popular feature of the summer Sundays.

One of the special treats for the missionary children are the times 'Uncle' Ken tells them fairy stories about seven little people only half-a-thumb high. He involves the children in the story which is ongoing, and created from his vivid imagination. In the 'Jhika Journal', a newsletter for the Murree Christian School Alumni Association, a 1967 graduate submits an article 'Thoughts on the Little People'.

When royalty comes to visit, the local lords
and ladies bring out their treasures—things too
valuable to leave lying around for use in mundane,

day-to-day activities. Treasures are things to glory in, things that make life special, things whose existence, use, appearance, taste, and smell make the moments take on a little more of a glow than if they didn't exist. And real treasures last a long time. They don't fade quickly—they can even be passed down from generation to generation.

Uncle Ken's visits were like visits of royalty to us. He brought us treasures, and in our little lives, we dragged out our own treasures, polished them up, and used them to make life more special. What were those treasures?

Uncle Ken sat with my sister Marty and me and told us stories—at least that is what any observant adult might have thought. His stories were about Little People that lived in his pockets. But in my view of the world, it wasn't the stories that were the treasures in and of themselves. It was the plots of the characters. I really couldn't tell you many specifics about Timothy or Gerald, and I really couldn't tell you any details at all about the stories. Those things were mere window dressing around the treasures that Uncle Ken brought us.

What he brought us that lasted, and continues to make life better, was something much deeper. Uncle Ken taught us about ourselves—the *real* Little People. He treated us children as if we were people with lives, imaginations, and value of our own. For those moments of his visits Timothy, Gerald, Marty and Dewey were intertwined. We were all the center of the universe. Whatever the story proposed was real, exciting, and valuable. Uncle Ken gave us our own imaginations as a treasure, and encouraged us to use them.

For me, he allowed me to imagine whatever I wanted, and didn't have any criticism at all. He just took that imagination and its imaginings and wove them into the stories. There's no greater treasure he could have brought into our lives!

Thanks, Uncle Ken
Dewey Christy

Summer on the Plains

Ken says that by nature, he is a hermit. A thousand years ago, he would have been chewing his cud on Mount Athos. Owing to a bypass of missionary procedures, which would surely have detected and rejected such a terrifying idiosyncrasy, he finds himself, with raised eyebrows and glazed daze, living on the campus of a boys' school in a house whose 21 outside doors are more frequently opening and closing than still.

Everyone has crosses to bear. Ken feels he probably has far too many for a normal person, but about the right number for a hermit. Some of the heaviest ones are servants and gadgets and birds.

Household servants are alright in their place; the trouble is; they are so often where Ken is. Somehow they seem to think that to be seen is to be appreciated. However, he admits that Ramat, the gardener, is an exception. It's because he only sees him on the thirtieth of each month. He is quite certain that the others work all the slower when he is present. They don't want to work so fast that they are out of sight before their industrious efforts are noticed. They are everywhere! Sheila will flick a spot of fluff from one corner of the room to the other for a full half hour while Ken waits patiently at the door. And then, when he turns away to the dining room… Lo! There she is—like the Hound of Heaven, polishing the mantelpiece.

Anything that doesn't work the first time is a gadget. It's

Ken's lowest term of contempt, applied indiscriminately to the Volkswagen or a blunt match. He could spend hours in a dream world of nostalgia where a horse and buggy supersedes a motor-driven car; a toasting fork relegates the pop-up toaster to limbo; a scrubbing board rings out its gravely tune on shirt buttons, and waffles have never been invented.

Summer is thus a time of mixed joy and sorrow. It's sad to be separated from Marie and two active little seven-year-olds when they go up to Murree. But it's no place for a hermit. For three months the house becomes an over-heated kiln where he's a willing burnt sacrifice. Mental rest is better than comfort. There are no servants walking in any of the 30 rooms. The dust settles slow and unruffled where it will. Sheila has a three-month rest. Ramat knows that his mistress won't appear until September to criticize his care of the garden. After all, plant growth is a natural process. Gadgets, as they break, are discarded. Orval provides Ken with food, either through a hole in the wall or one-and-a-half miles away.

The animal life doesn't bother Ken. He doesn't mind the bats or even the white ants nibbling steadily away at the roof beams above the bed. The rats and mice have become personal friends. It is ten days before he tracks down the squeaker that became caught in the door. The cockroaches hold country dances in the bathroom to celebrate his return from work, and spiders spin away like tops in all the corners.

It's the birds! He could have been a St. Francis except for the birds. He loves cuckoo-shrikes and flycatchers—it's the sparrows! And every one is a hen. They all have the homemaking instinct. First, they clean the cornices with frantic gyrations of their wings and scatter lumps of plaster all over the clean dust. Then in comes the grass for the nests. The bathroom would lead a stranger to believe that Ken eats grass. He could just about thatch a hut just by collecting what is all through the house.

Ken discovers that the vacuum cleaner is an interesting device. With the right pressure on the bedspread, it will remove the dust and plaster and termite droppings without disturbing the covers.

But it won't pick up grass! It jams. And those birds know it. How they get in eludes him. And how to get out eludes them. Ken feels they blame him because they can't find their way out. But he opens doors, blocks open the screens, closes curtains and waves his hands like a train-guard's flag. Those birds just laugh at him. It's not nice, being laughed at by birds. And why should *his* conscience be uneasy if they choose to starve? Why should *he* have to crumble biscuits into crumbs and put out saucers of water just because they don't know the way to go home? It would be a lonely summer except for the birds.

A year later, Ken is transferred to Taxila to build an operating block and two eye-wards. Once again, he's living in the Mission Hospital. In the evenings, little boys, with all the exuberance of youth, are flying paper kites and cavorting with them in spirit in the wild air. The wind, like a mournful lover, is sighing and sobbing in the shisham and cypress trees. Adults, in the refreshing cool of early evening, hazard a guess about how long until the rain comes—an hour, or three, or tomorrow? Little children wait expectantly for the first drops to spatter in the dust so they strip off ragged clothing and shoes and dance with blissful abandon in the torrents of rain while splashing through the puddles.

Until now the weather has been very still and sticky, over 100 degrees with humidity over 50 percent, so Ken has been sleeping on the roof. The slowly rising full moon casts its tender light over the sleepy city where all its various sounds are muted. An elderly Muslim, a friend of many years, tells Ken, "I hold you as my brother and your wife as my sister—you are as dear to me as any other members of my family." Ken realizes how hard it will be to go home when his and Marie's, hearts are at peace among these people who have become their people.

Timmy is a little mathematically confused. He says proudly, "I'm half English and half American and half Pakistani—why can't my skin be brown like the other children?"

Ken's mind travels back 18 years to the first Independence Day celebration. It was the first time he ever saw whole fields carpeted with white, a sea of praying men, rising and falling.

They were joyful, excited, a little fearful, giving thanks for their own country at last. In those days, tribesmen, armed to the teeth, crowded onto his rickety old truck whenever he came down from the hills towards the Indus River. With flashing eyes, they talked of taking Kashmir (and a little loot) now and Delhi in five years. Now, once again, he's hearing talk of fighting and wonders whether the tribesmen will be able to restrain themselves as the inevitable reports of atrocities begin to filter over the border.

A young man who was present at that Independence Day ceremony has just been to visit. Back then he was a sub-divisional officer who worked closely with Ken. He comes storming into Ken's office, tears running down his face, and tosses a Civil and Military Gazette on the desk. This is the same newspaper Rudyard Kipling published in Lahore. The headlines leave little doubt of the chaos on the plains. He blurts out, "Look what they're doing to our people! Just look what they're doing! They are beasts, just beasts!" He needs to protest to someone, anyone. His heart is just breaking. The news is of riots in an area likely to become part of India. The reports, in lurid prose, tell of pregnant Muslim women being slit open and the unborn children they carry ripped from their bodies. The tongues of infant children are cut so that they will never be able to recite their creed. Retaliation is inevitable—terror mounting on the back of terror. Ken tells Mohammed, "I'll prepare a bunker in the basement of my home at the hospital for your womenfolk."

A great tank battle is raging several miles away and the Indians are shelling the city. Fortunately, the expected assault on the city doesn't come. Ken prays for wisdom in High Places that a just settlement of the Kashmir question might be made once and for all.

A young Hindu carpenter working for Ken is acquitted of being a spy after having tried to slip over the border to persuade his 15-year-old wife to return to him. With smiling eyes, he tells Ken, "She will be returning any day now."

Ken is now bogged down in lawsuits. A lawsuit in Murree is to determine water rights on their property there. So far he has traveled 1,000 miles on this case without yet having been called to give evidence. The TB patients' ward should be complete and in use, but a neighbor brings a court injunction so that means several months of delay. Ken anticipates building on an empty plot nearby, but dangers of infection would cause him great loss.

Ken is grateful for church friends in England and America who have given generously so he can buy a truck. He has already traveled nearly 3,000 miles in it, and hasn't had a single breakdown. The vehicle was somewhat suspect as the rear axle had broken three times in the same place. But he is reassured when he gets stuck in a rice field up to the top of the hub caps for two hours. He emerges rather muddily none the worse for wear. It makes work so much easier, being able to cart a concrete mixer, or roofing supplies, stone, and cement directly to the site. Previously the only alternative was to use a bullock cart, change to the train, and then back to a bullock cart again. In a year or so he'll probably obtain permission to sell it and then it will be repaired for the very last time.

Missionaries and Humor

B eing a missionary is a deadly serious business, or is it? After all, the missionary enterprise is based on the eternal value of the human soul in God's economy and purpose.

You can hardly get more serious than that. People endure persecution, deprivation, often poverty, illness, and, for some, death in doing this work. The length of the first missionary term used to be seven years and then five years—long spells of time to be away from families and friends.

Strangely, the gift that enables so many to survive is probably not faith, or even grace, but the twin gifts of stubbornness and humor.

While in Karachi assisting and observing new missionary arrivals, Ken lists six gifts that a person needs to survive and be effective as a missionary. Not one of them directly relates to communion with God, but are traits of character that help people handle adversity. The initials spell the word CHRIST. The attributes are:

Common sense

Humor

Resilience of spirit

Integrity

Self-discipline

Tenacity

The Sialkot Mission is a mission par excellence. There isn't a better example in the country. It was in existence before the Indian Mutiny of 1857. Its people have been tested by fire. They have their own cemeteries where many graves are those of their children. They have dealt with diseases of all kinds, including smallpox, typhoid, and cholera. They labor in an area where malaria is a normal part of life. And they don't have the benefit of antibiotics, rapid transport, or ready medical attention.

Ken is observing the tail end of the Sialkot Mission. It's being phased out of existence in favor of a new co-operative relationship between the US mother church and the Synod of the Punjab. This will eventually become the Presbyterian Church of Pakistan.

The people Ken works with, Norval and Dorothy Christy, Orval and Lucy Hamm, Fred and Margie Stock, Bob and Rowena Tebbe, and John and Dorothy Wilder, just to name a few, laugh a lot. All kinds of private jokes circulate between them. They play practical jokes on each other, know each other's weaknesses, foibles, and idiosyncrasies, and bring a healthy rollicking humor to play on them. The newspaper they circulate among themselves, News Notes, not only gives news of the stations, but prevents anyone from feeling pompous or proud. Ken submits an article that illustrates his own twisted sense of humor.

So many things bug me, I know I must be abnormal.

Peanut butter is one. I don't know why I look like one big comfortable mother shell to all those detached and churned homeless nuts, but I do.

I don't like the stuff.

I don't like its smell, or its taste, or its appearance.

Whenever I get anywhere near it, it leaks over my clothes, my luggage, or my books with great spreading splotches.

So why is it that, whenever I go to Sialkot, I look like God's gift, a nut-crunchy traveling salesman, to deliver this stuff to some addict far removed and a long, hot journey away?

I have been willing to break friendship irreparably, to receive heaped curses, and have tried to turn a deaf ear to incessant requests. Still... this ill-favored concoction of George Washington Carver's finds itself secreted in my luggage or is anonymously thrust into my unsuspecting hands as my bus departs.

PLEASE don't bug me anymore, Lucy!

And Irv Lotze is another! I know I look soft,

but why does he always pick on me to deliver things?

I creep by CTS doors when I'm in Gujranwala lest he discover me and, putting his big warm arm around my shoulders, say "By the way..." Why does he always say, "By the way..."? It's not on my way; it's a great, almost insurmountable roadblock right dead center in the middle of my road.

"By the way, would you mind dropping off a refrigerator door handle we fixed? Leave it on the Nobles' back verandah." Then, having rung out a sullen acquiescence, he shows me a newly chromed handle attached to a glistening ten-cubic-foot 'minor' accessory.

It's the washing machine motor that really has fixed my doing errands for Irv. I've had long restless nights fleeing up endless roads in pursuit of a phantom bus propelled by a rear mounted washing machine motor agitating itself into a frenzy.

It began as usual. That big friendly arm around me. "By the way..." Later, I could just dimly recall being led like a sheep to the slaughter, to the grisly pile of mechanism in the CTS yard and then...blank!

When, eventually, the questions began, I desperately started the decoy ploy. I had left it for Wilbur to bring up in his car. He was sharp in retaliation and denial born of great experience, although I could see I left him uneasy and groping within his own gray matter.

The thought of explaining to Dorothy Christy I had left her washing machine motor, which she probably prized more than anything else she had ever possessed, on a Burhan Transport bus was frightening.

I tried the old standby. If anything is missing, try Bob Noble's back verandah. That verandah is the focus of the mission. Bob was quick in affirming, as a principle, his complete mental detachment from anything that might be put on his back verandah, or, for that matter, taken off it. Certainly there was no tortured mechanism there with enough energy to propel a toothbrush, let alone a washing machine.

Desperation leads to desperate measures. I went over to the attack. I told Irv I couldn't even remember seeing that washing machine motor; that I wasn't sure washing machines had motors, and that even if I had seen it, I certainly would not have made myself dirty touching it."

The missing bit of machinery was eventually found on Byron Haines back verandah where Irv himself had delivered it!

Another example of missionary humor is the Sialkot Mission's choice of tunes for the Psalms. The church service for the local citizens needs to have songs they can sing in their native language. For the Presbyterians from America they are obviously going to come from the Psalter, the arrangement of the Psalms to music.

The Psalms are first translated into Urdu, but it isn't until they're translated into the true vernacular, Punjabi, that the Psalms become the folksongs, the spirituals of the church. Now comes the need for tunes THAT ARE EASY TO SING. Musically minded missionaries wander through the Sialkot bazaars, listening carefully to the street singers. The lyrics are lewd and bawdy. It doesn't matter, they are the popular tunes of the day, and the new words to be used will long outlast the originals. This works well. The tunes, usually sung to repeated couplets, complement the words of the Psalms. All 150 Psalms soon have tunes THAT ARE EASY TO SING. The words are becoming locked into the collective memory of the Punjabi church.

The Synod of the Punjab is the first to use the Psalter. As other churches grow, they adopt the same Psalter. All Punjabi Christians, Catholic or Protestant, sing the same tunes. The very last Psalm is a whimsical touch from home, illustrating missionary humor to the full. It uses the music from "Oh, my darling, Oh my darling, Oh my darling Clementine." The Punjabi words can be sung quite lustily to this tune.

Missionaries will get themselves into trouble, but always, along with sound advice and good practical help, there is empathetic laughter with the thought "There, but for the grace of God, go I."

Taxila Christian Hospital

Taxila Christian Hospital began serving rural patients in 1922 with quality, low-cost healthcare. Although it's a general hospital, it's more widely known for preventing blindness and restoring sight. It's the largest eye clinic in the world. Each spring, patients pour in from the mountains and plains. The prolonged winter rains, while promising an excellent harvest of dwarf Mexican wheat, have prevented travel to the hospital. Now the influx of patients is again underway. Some of them, nearly blind, lay trusting hands on the shoulders of sighted companions. Following the removal of cataracts, they eagerly anticipate the miracle of restored sight. By the end of the year a new operating block will be opened with three operating rooms instead of one. The doctors wonder whether they will be able to achieve 7,000 cataract operations in one year.

All four doctors are busy. Ernest Lall heads the team, and is constantly active. This morning he begins at three a.m. helping his wife in the O.R. By seven, about 140 cataract operations are done. Ken, although an engineer and not a doctor, arrives at the hospital at four to help with the surgery patients until his own building work begins at eight. Marie is in uniform, working in the clinic and making rounds. She no longer works in the operating room, but Dorothy Christy holds on valiantly like the trooper she is.

At eleven Pamela Lall, 230 eye operations already behind her, moves to the clinic where she'll work until four. Ernest will operate on general patients when the tables are available, and then he, too, sees patients in the clinic.

Norval Christy walks three miles on rounds, before clinic, checking on 800 inpatients. By next week that will swell to nearly 1100. Sixty patients sleep on the operating block verandah, heads covered with cloth to avoid flies. 70 patients are in the incomplete Oxfam ward. Ken's workmen are squeezed out as beds are placed over partially completed concrete molds and against plasterers' scaffolding. The three new verandah wards can each hold 40 patients; the older wards hold their full complement of 100.

Dr. Eileen sees the women general patients. With gentleness, she unravels problems across language barriers, and the haziness as to the nature of the complaint or its duration. The foreign nurses, Nicky and Judy, who soon return home, say with a smile what they cannot with words. In the women's ward they trim eyelashes and a relative, sitting in error on the patient's bed, is likely to be shorn before she can blink.

In September the Men's general ward, donated by the British charity Oxfam, will be opened. It's customary to have a spotless new building for opening day, but it was more in keeping with

Taxila tradition to have the building already in use.

Jacqui, God's gift of an English secretary to Ken, takes the bedlam of the season in her stride, reporting, "Yes, all went well this morning except when a patient had a severe coronary just after his first injection. The other patients waiting on the O.R. floor became quite uneasy."

This morning, Siddique came with his club-footed baby. The father's appearance gives the impression that he is a Greek colonist left behind many centuries ago in the northern mountains. He's confident. "The Lall doctor (Ernest) can fix foot. Will he cut it off and put it back straight? The baby will have only one foot if he doesn't stick it on. Is it true it costs 400 rupees?" This is four month's wages, but the child is admitted for the operation.

On the verandah is a cameo to treasure. The tailor, cross-legged, trims a girl's new blue shirt. He chats, not being understood, to two ragged little girls from the sparsely settled hills in the North West Frontier. For some weeks, carrying themselves with unconscious grace and childish innocence, they have occasionally been in Taxila begging. With eyes like saucers they see new clothes being made for *them*. Yesterday, before putting on the finished garments, they were bathed (OH, the dirt!) and their clean hair braided into tight little braids. And Gogo, with inexpressible wonder in her eyes, thinks her cup might overflow when she is given a 50-cent pair of plastic sandals.

Ken has had some strange tasks during his years in Taxila. On one occasion he even serves as treasurer for a mosque when the congregation couldn't find anyone trustworthy. Now he oversees the operation of a brick kiln. Mud bricks are made by the thousands in hand molds. A man and his wife can perhaps make 1,500 a day earn $1.50 for their efforts. The sun-dried bricks are placed in the kiln for seven days, after which time they can be removed for sale. The profits from the bricks are intended to help finance new campus construction at Chitan College in Rawalpindi. This is another project for which Ken has just been given responsibility.

Richard and Kathleen

September 1969 – February 1970

Ken's parents plan an extended visit in 1969 to help out while Marie is in England receiving medical treatment. Ken's mother keeps a diary of daily events for the full five months they are there. It gives a glimpse into the busy life of the extraordinary man that Ken is. His wide range of activities and responsibilities are staggering.

The trip does not get off to a good start. Their plane is delayed seven hours and they don't arrive in Karachi, Pakistan until late the next evening. They stay the night in Karachi, and arrive in Lahore at 9.30 a.m. Ken is there to meet them and finds a place for them to stay for the night as he is working in Lahore. They will travel on to Gujranwala in the morning. There they are met by Ed and Audrey Carlson, who drive them to Sialkot. The Sialkot Convention is in session and they attend the afternoon meeting.

Ken is driving his parents to Rawalpindi where they will pick up Tim and Colin and go to the airport to meet three nurses. 20 miles from Pindi, the rear axle of the truck breaks. Ken leaves his parent with the truck, and thumbs a ride into town. He tells Tim and Colin, "Go to the airport to meet the three nurses." He asks his good friend Byron Haines, "Will you take me to my broken down vehicle and tow it back to Pindi for repair?" Byron invites all of them—Ken, his parents, the two boys, and the three nurses to have dinner with him before they take a bus to Taxila. It's 10:30 p.m. when they arrive. Richard and Kathleen are exhausted and fall right into bed.

In the morning, Kathleen looks out the bedroom window to a beautiful garden carpeted with flowers. Most of the day is spent in unpacking. Norval, the eye doctor at the hospital, and his wife, Dorothy come to visit. They are pleased to have three nurses to help with the load. Ken has been doing the household chores and spends his day washing clothes and baking cakes—four of them—and Kathleen exclaims, "They are absolutely *Superb!*"

Sunday morning, Richard and Kathleen go to the English speaking church service at the hospital. Ken and the nurses attend the one held in the home of Bilquis. Ken's close friend, Dave Mitchell, leads the evening service.

Tim and Colin have to return to school on Monday and their grandmother has made her famous yeast buns for them to take along. Ken will be working in Sialkot for a few days and the nurses have gone to Pindi, so Richard and Kathleen are on their own. This is the time Piskey, the boys' dog decides to have her puppies! Richard puts her in a box and takes it into Ken's room. By 3:30 she has delivered *six* puppies.

Ken goes to bed at 9:00 and gets up at the crack of dawn. He has his parents up at 5:30 to have tea in the garden. Richard and the three nurses make a short trip ten miles north to see a new dam and visit some ruins. Kathleen spends her days keeping the house tidy, cooking, writing letters home, and, when she has a spare moment, reading books. Ken and his parents always enjoy the Wednesday evening Bible study with Bilquis in her home.

The middle of October, Kathleen makes plans for a big celebration. She spends all morning cooking. Nicky, one of the nurses helps in the afternoon. Tim and Colin are down from school. They look forward to playing with their Samoyed dogs, but have to take a bath first. The day of the party, Kathleen is busy arranging furniture, setting tables, and completing other last-minute preparations. It is an elaborate affair—27 people have been invited. The festivities go on until 11:00 with everyone chatting and playing games. It is obviously something pretty special to keep Ken up so late, but the reason remains a mystery.

The first week of October, Marie returns home. She is tired and has a cold, but otherwise okay. Tim and Colin come down from school on the weekend to see her.

Audrey Carlson invites Kathleen to come to Gujranwala to attend a women's missionary conference. Dr. Lall, from the hospital, will go with her. They leave at 7:00, drive to the train station in Pindi, and take the 8:30 train to Wazirabad. From there, they take a bus to Gujranwala. Finally, a tonga drops them off with Audrey's family in time for lunch. Kathleen is quite taken with their darling little two-year-old boy, Kurt. She tells Audrey about their trip, "That was some train ride! Unlike any I have ever experienced before."

Ken is running a high fever and the doctor is called. After three days, Ken attempts to get up, but has had nothing to eat, and is too weak. On the fifth day, the doctor says he may get up for just one hour. Ken uses the time to pay his workers their wages out in the garden, and then spends another hour or two in the lounge chair by the fire. He never is good at following doctor's orders. Feeling a little better, he eats a bit of soup— the first food he's had in five days. It's another five days before he feels well enough to go to work. Although he's doing better, he's still a long way from being well.

Although it's Thanksgiving, Kathleen can sit in the garden and enjoy the 'glorious' sunshine. The English don't celebrate Thanksgiving, but the next night they enjoy a feast at the home of Norval and Dorothy Christy. Two missionary teachers from Kabul, Afghanistan are there, and they invite Richard to go back with them to spend a few days enjoying their city. While he's away, Kathleen goes with Ken to pick up Tim and Colin in Murree. The ride is a little more adventurous than she would like as they get hit by an Army truck. The damage is minor and they are able to complete their journey.

When Kathleen goes shopping with Marie in Wah, she is delighted to actually see meat *without* flies in an enclosed market. Richard enjoys walking down to the train station. He wants to get pictures of eye patients arriving. Marie, Tim, and Colin are now fighting the flu, but the rest of them have miraculously kept well. One Sunday, Ken's parent's decide to attend an Urdu church service. They don't speak the language so it's uncertain how much they can understand. Although the hymns are from the Psalms, they aren't in English.

One of the doctors who works at the hospital, Dr. Eileen, invites Ken's parents and the three nurses to have lunch at her parent's home. They live in Pindi. Ken offers to drive them. The unreliable truck breaks down once again, and Ken takes a bus back to the hospital to get a car so they can complete their journey. The fare is a typical Pakistani meal and Kathleen finds it 'lovely'.

Ken has people knocking at his door for medicine. A man brings his son who is too sick to stand and Ken sends them to the hospital to see Dr. Eileen. Three of the men who come to Ken for pills don't take them until sundown because this is a month of fasting for all Muslims.

The Sunday before Christmas, the whole family attends a carol service in the chapel. Ken, Marie, Tim, Colin, and the three nurses sing a carol for the judges. The Christy family also sings a carol. Marie and Dorothy Christy are the judges.

Marie sends for her former servant, Khan Zaman, to help with final Christmas preparations. He's wonderful in the kitchen and when he arrives, her mind is set at ease about the cooking. For afternoon tea he bakes marvelous doughnuts and cinnamon rolls. Kathleen is busy wrapping presents for Tim, Colin, and her husband. Ken gives new clothes to his workmen. He buys 37 overcoats and lays them out on the lawn. Each man can choose one, but the Kohistanis choose first because they are the poorest.

For Christmas Eve the ladies are all giving each other 'posh' hairdos. Kathleen is wearing her blue lace dress and likes the hairdo Nicky and Judy gave her. Dinner is a typical English mean—roast chicken, mashed potatoes, peas, carrots, hot tomato juice, and the traditional Christmas pudding for dessert along with coffee. In addition to Ken's family of six, there is the Christy family of five, the four Mitchells, Bilquis and her grandson, Mahmud, the three nurses— Judy, Cecilia, and Nicky—and four new volunteers—Bill McPherson, Dave Morrison, Judy Harvey, and Jacqui Rubin. All 24 sing carols until 8:30.

A Question of Time

Marie goes to register for a sewing class. She is only able to get the form. Her companion regrets that another visit will be necessary. Nothing to regret. In Pakistan, obtaining the form counts as a very satisfactory conclusion to a day's work. Jonathan Scopes made 27 visits to the Passport office and innumerable visits to the bank, the police, and various and sundry other places, merely to get a reentry visa to come back should he leave the country.

It's all a question of time and priorities. The passport officer feels that you have come to exchange courtesies and make acquaintance. When you call on a friend, it's enough to have called and shared pleasantries, news of your children, and what you think Russia will do next. Any attempt to include a reason for the errand can spoil a God-given occasion to relax and enjoy the passage of time.

Ken's father finds this approach to life disconcerting. Richard is a rather fastidious man. He has come from a business in Regent Street, where neither mail nor the train wait for any man, and a minute will make all the difference. Now, in a Punjabi village, he tries to find out when to post the mail. It's suggested he put it in the box. It will probably go out sometime. For Richard, such casualness is close to heresy. After all, there must be a time, or hopefully times, when the mail will go out. There isn't. He decides to walk down alongside the railway tracks from the hospital to the post office.

His entrance is disconcerting. The mail, either incoming or outgoing—but probably both—is scattered on the floor in wild confusion. Customers and clerks try to skirt around the mail or, more delicately, remove their shoes before walking on it.

Richard picks his way around people bending over trying to read Arabic script. He wonders how, if they don't read English, they can ever sort out *his* mail. His mail, having traveled six thousand hazardous miles to get here, and undoubtedly carrying messages of importance, is obviously being sorted onto mailing bound for some illiterate hovel in Khanpur or Faizabad whose residents are desperate for the material to kindle a fire.

He assesses the task at hand. The first thing is to establish communication. Easier said than done. A clerk on his knees looks up and motions him to a chair. The wicker chair has no seat in it. Traces of bamboo hang from the rim of the frame in dejection as though the chair has just been sat on by an elephant. A quick glance confirms there's no other seat.

Richard decides to remain standing. This, however, implies that the staff of the post office is being discourteous in causing the honored guest to remain standing. The sorting of mail continues without pause. The clerk looks up briefly and again motions to the chair. Richard pauses and then gingerly eases himself onto the rim of the chair. It creaks painfully. He tries to work out whether the mail is being sorted by size or color. There appears to be little or no reference to the address. He has a growing sense of horror, or fantasy. He thinks of all the urgent mail he's written since his arrival that by now should have reached its various destinations. If any of his letters have even gotten out of this place, it would be a miracle.

He clears his throat, smiles nervously, and prepares to launch into battle. "Postmaster?" he ventures.

It's as though he's thrown a stone into a flock of pigeons. All activity among the scattered papers stops. All heads turn towards him. The clerk who motioned him to the chair points to a gray-haired old dodderer who should have been pensioned off

20 years ago. This man is the only one not sorting through the piles of mail.

The old man is engrossed in trying to dampen a rubber stamp on a bone dry stamp pad that has been worn smooth and polished by many thumbprints. He pours some dregs of tea from a tiny cup with a chipped edge onto the stamp pad. He then tries to persuade its absorption by working it into the pad with the blunt end of a pencil. He's more absorbed in his task than the tea is. He upends the pad to drain off the surface. Even Richard becomes fascinated with the struggle. 'Old Father Time' looks up, smiles satisfaction and presses his rubber stamp with all his force onto the pad. He looks at it, breathes on it hard a couple of times, and is ready to try using it again. He presses it down on a large envelope—hard.

By now all the staff, caught up in fascination with the process, are staring in amazement along with Richard. The word 'URGENT' appears ever so faintly on the envelope. The old man indicates by his shrug that he's done his best, but in the face of such tribulation how could he hope for more?

Having caught 'Methuselah's' attention, Richard isn't going to let go. "Stamps?" he smiles brightly. The old man understands. He's the linguist in the place. "Kitne?" he responds and then, seeing the blank look of incomprehension. he changes languages. "How much?"

Here Richard makes a mistake. He assumes that those two words imply a companion soul with whom there is perfect understanding. That is not so. The Postmaster, for it is indeed he, has only a limited grasp of this particular language. His skills lie in Urdu, Pushto, Hindko, and Punjabi. It's a rare occasion when his English fluency is tested. Both men, as the conversation progresses, strain for understanding. A word here and a word there, and a great deal of mental agility, suggest communication is about 50 percent correct, and 50 percent wrong. Now all the clerks have joined in to assist in the progress—pooling their limited knowledge into the increasing confusion.

Ken's father doesn't know whether "How much?" refers

to the value of each stamp or the quantity of each stamp he wants. It doesn't, in the end, matter. It was a rhetorical question, a conversational opener having no reality. The post office has no stamps. Richard works his way through the pages of the copybook where, in more prosperous times, stamps would have been sorted according to their value. 'Methuselah' demonstrates with a shrug of sadness and successive open, empty pages that, no matter what number Richard might hazard, the answer is always the same. "There are no stamps." He's anxious to please but, after all, what can he do?

Richard is absolutely amazed. What kind of post office is this? After all, the job of a post office is to sell stamps. How can the mail go out without stamps? Without stamps, the whole commerce and life of Taxila will grind to a halt.

The Postmaster spreads his hands wide, palms up. "Sir, you must remember, we are a very poor country." There is insufficient mutual comprehension to allow this discussion on Pakistan's economy to proceed further.

Ken's father launches into another area of concern. An hour has already passed. He has his pencil and paper ready. By now he's expressing himself as simply as he knows how, slowly and clearly. "What time is the mail?" Again, more clearly, for there has been no sign of dawning comprehension. "What time does the post go out?" The answer is less than satisfying. "Sometimes ten o'clock, sometimes eleven o'clock, sometimes 12:00, sometimes tomorrow, or the next day."

Richard withholds any comment as he reflects that this is certainly no way to run a post office. He gradually manages, with much mutual smiling, nodding of heads, and shaking of heads, to piece together enough bits of information to determine the routine of sorting the mail for dispatch.

The Postmaster produces a small cup with a chipped edge filled with hot creamy tea from the tea shop next door. He flicks the fly out of the tea with his pencil and passes it over to Richard. By now they are as friends who have known each other for years.

The schedule for outgoing mail is variable because the Khyber

Mail train is unreliable. Its due time is 9:15. It usually arrives about 10:30. However, sometimes it's early, but more often it's closer to noon. On occasion, it's been so late it failed to stop and just rushed through the station gaining speed for the climb to Margalla. The post office has its own special, unique routine. If the bicycle tires aren't punctured, and it's available, someone can make it to the station when they hear the train coming. It's more difficult when the Postmaster is the only one there. His hearing is impaired and he's not secure on a bicycle. The other staff try to be present to avoid that eventuality. Most times it works out fine. But, if ever they miss the train, the next day is doubly difficult, and the odds twice as long. There's twice as much mail to move in a short space of time. However, this staff at Taxila Post Office are loyal and dedicated postmen who will stop at nothing to make sure that the mail goes through.

Richard, like his son, is no slouch. He sees through the whole problem in a flash. The answer lies, not at the post office, but at the railway station. Promising to return, he makes another half mile to the railway station. He requests a railway timetable and is directed to a seller of books with garish paper covers. "Timetable?" he asks, mimicking the pronunciation of the booking clerk. It's a word instantly recognized. A booklet with a picture of a steam train at full speed is produced. Some coins are taken from the selection offered in Richard's outstretched palm. He now possesses a full timetable of all trains on Pakistan railroads arriving at and leaving from Karachi—in Arabic script.

He turns to Ken for help. Now there is a notice in Copperplate handwriting stuck on the window of the post office. It advises the public in English that collections of mail will be made from this postbox at 9:42 a.m., 12:30 p.m. and 5:32 p.m. each day except Sundays and public holidays. Ken's father has made his contribution to the development of the East. He's made many friends in the process and the oxcart wheels continue to creak and squeak into the night as they have always done.

On Christmas morning, Richard and Kathleen are awakened at 7:00 by Ken and the boys loudly singing, "Oh, Come All Ye

Faithful" right outside the bedroom door. Wearing their dressing gowns, they make their way downstairs into the lounge for tea and devotions. Then they open presents. At 10:30 Ken, the boys, and his parents go to church which is decorated with faded flags. The church is packed full and nearly all the women are wearing new pants, chemise, and scarves. Marie and four of the girls attend a church in Pindi for an English service. After church, Ken prepares tea and it's time to go to the hospital Christmas dinner which is served outside. Everyone brings their own plate, silverware, and glass. The meal is curry and rice, and sweet rice for dessert. The doctors and hospital staff do the serving and everyone who lives on the hospital compound is invited. Ken takes the nurses to Wah to say, "Happy Christmas" to their friends and Kathleen spends the time clearing away all the wrapping paper. The day finishes with evening devotions.

The next day is Boxing Day in England, but not in Pakistan. It's the day unwanted presents are returned to the store. Richard goes to the hospital to do some painting. The weather is perfect so Kathleen takes a book and sits in the garden to read. Ken isn't feeling well, but he dresses in his Father Christmas suit complete with whiskers, and goes to Wah with a bag of toys for the boys there.

The New Year comes in quietly with no celebrations. However, 1970 will bring much change and bigger challenges. Ken has completed the foundation for the men's ward at the hospital. The following week, Marie, Tim, Colin, Kathleen, and two of the volunteers catch the train to Lahore. They have an enjoyable visit with missionary friends from Denmark, Piet and Elise Born and their three girls.

In the morning, Marie takes Kathleen shopping at Hildas. She wants to buy gifts to take back to England. She finds beautiful tea cozies made by Pakistani women. A haircut and shampoo costs more than she expected—39 schillings and 9 pence. But it is worth it. She thoroughly enjoys the lunch at Shezan's restaurant. In the evening she spends time with the three little girls while Elise goes to choir practice.

The next two days, she and Marie walk through the bazaar and take one last look in all the shops without buying anything except food for the journey home. She is tired, but has enjoyed the change from her daily routine.

There is no space available when four tourists arrive. One stays with Dr. Eileen, one with Mark, and the other two in the Land Rover. January 24th is Richards's birthday and Marie bakes a cake that says, 'Happy Birthday Granddad.' All too soon it is February 11th and time for Richard and Kathleen to return home. Goodbyes are said and Ken takes them to the train station. Some of his Pakistani friends are there with beautiful garlands for Richard and Kathleen. Ken will go with them as far as Karachi, and they take the 9:00 train. They share a compartment with three Pakistani men. It's an all day, all night journey. They enjoy several trays of tea and one cooked meal. They arrive in Karachi at midday on the 12th and take a taxi to the orphanage where Ken and Marie once worked. The old ladies are so pleased to see him! Then they go to the travel agent where they leave their luggage. One of Ken's friends gives them lunch. The travel agent will take them to the boat so they say their goodbyes to Ken. On board ship, they unpack, have dinner, and go to bed. The ship sails at midnight.

A New Challenge

Ken has been asked to leave his building work in Taxila and serve as Principal of the Christian Technical Training Center in Gujranwala. CTTC is an institution for the equipping of young men as wage earners and Christian laymen. Graduates from this school are trained manual workers and rarely have difficulty finding work. Irv Lotze, the current principal has been granted a furlough. You remember Irv—the one with the big friendly arm who says, "By the way…"

This venture into education from civil engineering and building will be refreshing, exciting, and certainly challenging. Having no experience of education this will offer many challenges, not the least of which will be just keeping the ship afloat. Almost every student comes from a poor family. Many of their families are tied to the feudal system by poverty and crushing debts. After two or three years of training, boys from sweeper or peasant families are earning four or five times the pittance their parents earn. But each student needs at least $12 a month and all the scholarship funds have been exhausted. For the past several years, churches and friends overseas have provided this support. The challenge before Ken is to convince these supporters to continue supplying the resources needed. And new supporters will be needed as one of the goals is to increase enrollment from 60 boys to 250. This challenge amounts to nearly a million dollars. Ken looks forward to seeing God's faithfulness displayed in large things as well as small.

In October 1970 the move to Gujranwala marks a change-point in Ken's life. God now has Ken in the place the voice told him about in 1949. He is in a different land, among people of a different culture and a different faith, and he is working among boys. It has taken 20 years of difficult and diverse training to bring Ken to this point. Now, instead of the three years asked of him, he will spend 20 years here fulfilling the purposes God intended for him from the beginning.

Ken spends long hours at the school every day. Rising bright and early at five, he works for a couple of hours before taking a break to return home for breakfast. All students are required to attend assembly before classes start. A different member of staff is responsible for giving the message each morning. Ken, sitting at his desk piled deep with paperwork, is reminded that it is his turn today. He has forgotten so hasn't given any thought to what he should say. On the short walk from his office to the assembly hall, he decides on a scripture. Giving an interpretation of that, he explains how students and teachers can apply the wisdom gleaned from God's word in their daily lives. Neither teachers nor students are aware that his message is entirely extemporaneous.

While the workmen Ken supervises take their lunch break, he takes the opportunity for a half-hour power nap. Stretching out on the cement floor, hands behind his head for a pillow, he is quickly asleep. He needs no alarm to wake him, the ants crawling over his face, arms and legs rouse him. Carefully brushing the tiny insects off him, (they are God's creation after all) Ken is refreshed and ready for the rest of the day.

There have been problems in the past with neighborhood boys climbing the fence that surrounds the campus. They don't want to cause trouble; they just want to use the basketball court. Ken feels there is no reason why they shouldn't be allowed access to the court. He promptly orders the fence to be demolished. There does need to be an indication of the school boundary, however. Ken's solution to this is to build a short wall of open, octagonal shaped concrete blocks. The design is Ken's own idea and lends an atmosphere of openness to the campus.

Each day at three o'clock, without fail, Ken stops whatever he's doing and walks to the house where he finds bright little Amy Jo waiting for him on the verandah. She has come to have afternoon tea with 'Uncle' Ken. She is always greeted with "Hello, Sweetheart!" On February 14th she gives him a Valentine card that becomes his lasting treasured memory of her. Not too many years later, her life is cut tragically short by a brain tumor, but not before she has found happiness with Dave and given birth to Kiran Hope moments before she dies.

Ken faces many challenges, some heartbreak mixed with joy, during the time in Gujranwala. He envisions and completes projects others would not dare undertake. But his perfect, unwavering trust in God's provision and guidance allows him to step out in faith to fulfill the purposes of God.

Another New Address

Ken has always appreciated his supporters. It doesn't matter if the support comes in the form of monetary gifts, letters, or volunteers who come to work alongside for a few days, weeks, or months. He knows God's hand is behind it all. He regularly writes a newsletter to keep them informed of progress.

One Sunday afternoon he sits on the porch of their new home in Gujranwala. He always enjoys the view. Behind the broad-leaved frangipani and the umbrella leaves arching over bunched bananas, the grey, smooth trunk of the eucalyptus trees soar skyward. From the spiked leaves of the tall palm in the grassy garden hang a score of weaver bird nests. Vultures trace circles in the sky overhead. The nearby hostel, crowded with boys, murmurs with conversation and the occasional lilt of a song. The gospel team of trainees on hired bicycles makes its way to outlying villages.

This is their 20th new home in 15 years. Three days ago they returned to Taxila for the furniture. This meant wrapping and packing glass and other fragile items, hoping they would get through unscathed. Yesterday the trucks finally arrived. One gaily painted truck still had reminders of its last load— water buffaloes. By noon both trucks were loaded and packed. Hopefully everything will arrive safely traveling 150 miles south over the million bumps and bounces. Marie goes by train while Ken catches one of the faster 'thrill a minute' station wagons.

The boys from the hostel unload everything, by the light of an oil lamp, into a garage riddled with white ants. By 9:30 the task is done and they can attend to an unexpected guest from Pasrur.

The place is infested with termites. Every morning Marie finds a shovel of dirt pushed away from the thick mud walls. She goes hunting for the queen. There's a large hole in the wall and another deep in the floor when she finally finds her. It looks like an ant head attached to a gross slug-like body. However, this is only a minor victory. The fine mud tunnels continue to appear through cracks in the walls, around the door posts, and lintels. Marie is constantly checking her cupboards to make sure those enemies aren't among the paper linens.

This new home is a gracious house—large, spacious and high-ceilinged as befits a dwelling from days before electricity. When an inner wall seemed likely to collapse under the weight of a mud-plastered tile roof, the roof was propped and the wall replaced with bricks and mortar.

Colin and Tim are now 13. One of them sends a heart-wrenching letter. He is ready for the winter break. "I've had a pretty hard term. It has weighed me down. I am exhausted. This is my last letter. See you in one week and four days." Marie is busy preparing rooms for them. They will arrive Friday.

Election fever is in the air. About 23 parties have entered the race, using multi-colored flags and symbols such as scales, swords, scissors, and airplanes to catch the eye of illiterate voters. Ken's concern is whether government instructions to close educational institutions until after Christmas to avoid disturbance applies to their school also. Some tactful discussions with officials will be needed.

The flooding in East Pakistan has prompted quick and generous sympathetic response from poverty to poverty. The drama group at the school is rehearsing a program to raise funds for flood relief. The boys and staff remember their own Punjab floods and have given generously from their limited income.

The Technical Training Center will be a challenging place to work, but it will be thrilling to see God provide for the needs.

The development plan to enlarge to 250 students will require more than $700,000. Ken sends a letter to friends in Europe and the States who may be able to help. It's already a thrill to see individual scholarships beginning to be provided for boys needing them. And it's a thrill to see God providing staff—two English lads and a couple from Pakistan to teach classes, an Irish couple to work in the hostel, and a summer visitor who may return with his wife. Ken looks for, and expects to find, Christian Pakistani staff for higher positions in the Center to prepare for a time when foreign help might not be possible.

Next summer they will need more hostel accommodations for the 65 new boys he expects to enroll. And expanded classroom and teaching facilities will also be needed. But Ken feels that so many needs will make them rich. He has seen in the past how God is faithful to provide every need.

Ken is refreshed as he anticipates Christmas. Each year His Advent seems to say more to the needs of this troubled world and mean more to those who know why He came. This Christmas, with all its happiness and festivity, reaches into his heart. It transforms his deepest needs into enduring blessings."

Inayat

Since the move to Gujranwala, insistent knocking at the door has become all too familiar. This time it is so insistent, it demands immediate attention.

Standing on the verandah is a gaunt, ragged man. Clustered around him are all his children. The oldest girl, not more than nine or ten, carries a baby on her hip. The child has matchstick legs, a distended stomach, and a badly infected hand. The children are thin, dirty, and barefoot. The man is incomprehensible, speaking a dialect that even confuses Punjabis. Ken doesn't yet understand that Inayat is a confused and confusing man who rarely succeeds in going in less than two directions at once. He's begging for food and help.

Maybe Ken should have given them food and left it at that, but the kids look so lost and the baby is sick. He doesn't know he's adopting a son and seven grandchildren. Nor does he realize how this man will twist him and Marie around his finger for the next 15 years. Inayat instantly adopts them as his parents without seeking their consent. Before they know what's happening, they become *his* servants.

Years later, Inayat still knocks insistently at least two or three times a day. He won't do anything until he gets Ken's specific advice. He tries to follow it as literally as his limited abilities and confused thinking of his mind allows.

His children understandably show no signs of academic achievement. Wherever the bottom of the class is, they are there or lower. They seem to be in second grade permanently while their friends pass on from middle school to high school. They have beaten, in their engaging way, the most dedicated teachers. For a while they are all in the home for poor children in Pasrur.

His teen-age daughter, Rani, goes to a school in Sialkot and proves to be an insurmountable scholastic challenge to teachers with decades of experience. Parveen goes to Sangla Hill instead and her unique, incomprehensibility becomes a standard by which the lowest level of intelligence for children is measured. Buta comes to the Christian Technical Training Center at the age of 13 and inaugurates the program for boys who can't learn anything, or hardly anything. Kala and Nikki are still at Pasrur, valiantly following in the footsteps of their siblings. Anwar and Rakho, an older son and daughter, are obviously the models for the younger ones.

Strangely, Inayat seems born out of his time. He should have been born before the invention of paper or police forces. He's a kind of Charlie Chaplin of the Punjab, a wistful illiterate, somehow forever caught up in events beyond his comprehension.

The local superintendent of police is a kindly man. It has cost the police hundreds of rupees these past few months. Ever since

Inayat heard that the man who ran off with his wife seven years ago has been arrested for stealing a water buffalo in a village nearby, he has used every wile at his disposal, and a few judicious lies, to help his case along. With frequent appeals to Ken for a letter to the deputy commissioner here, or the superintendent of police there, he practices his own brand of patience that makes the persistent widow seem like a fly-by-night. He eventually succeeds in having his wife and her only surviving child, out of five born to her, brought to Gujranwala by the police.

Inayat is Catholic. Sometimes he and most likely Father Paul also, have wished that he were not. An ecumenical grouping of five—the Presbyterian pastor, Padri Anwar, Father Paul, Ken, and the Muslim superintendent of police—now squat down with the woman to persuade her to rejoin her family who are standing watching. Inayat' pleas and the tears of the children she has deserted have already failed. She is hard-faced and bitter. "No, I will only come back to my family if they will all become Muslim." There is little religious significance in this. It's her way of saying no. It enrages her children. Rakho, a vixen, spits contemptuously on the floor, uses a few choice expletives, and declares, "This woman is not my mother. My mother is dead."

Now the next problem. If there is to be no wife, who is going to cook the chapattis, the bread of life, for Inayat? Conjugal bliss for Inayat seems to define itself through this question. Can Inayat marry again? One could hardly wish such an unequal encounter on any woman. Even though his wife's change of faith seems to nullify the earlier marriage, would the Catholic Church agree?

Now comes the brightest idea of Inayat's life. Marry off Buta—he must be nearly 16, possibly even 17. Then Buta's wife can cook the chapatis. But Inayat is a very poor man. He has another, even more brilliant idea. Inspiration seems to come in surges. Marry off Rani at the same time and save the cost of a wedding.

For the past few weeks there have been frequent comings and goings. Ken finds a young man in Pindi who is willing to marry Rani. In nearby Wah, Inayat finds a boy whom he prefers to be Rani's husband. And he finds a woman to be Buta's wife. The completion of the whole operation will come from the same family.

Somehow Ken gets thrust upon him the unwelcome job of being Inayat's banker. At the most inappropriate times, Inayat seeks Ken out, and thrusts grubby notes, saved from his pay as a laborer or night watchman, into Ken's hand. This nest-egg, carefully accumulated and guarded, is for eventual deposit on one of the houses Ken is building in Brend colony.

Inayat raids his fund to the tune of 800 rupees to buy a dowry for Rani. Rakho and Inayat comb the bazar for bargains. They buy quilts, mattresses, velvet cushions, pillows, bedspreads, tins for flour, and the big metal dowry box to hold everything. The seamstress is working on the perfect dress to make Rani the most beautiful bride ever.

Buta, on his part, has borrowed tools to supplement his own and is busy making chairs and other furniture to provide for his future bride.

An Incredible Play
at the Theater

Today is Saturday, a day to relax and reflect that all preparations are in place for the *big* day tomorrow— the beginning of the week long wedding celebrations. However, the events that unfold themselves are too bizarre to record in normal prose. Settle yourselves into front row seats, center stage, at the local village theater. Watch what is certain to be an organizational disaster—comedy mixed with pathos.

Prologue: Buta has a classmate in the carpentry shop who is a bad influence. Chita, known as the Cat, has a brother who is a murderer, and Chita is not much better. Daku is a thief who keeps the whole neighborhood terrorized. In his spells out of jail, he brandishes a long knife and robs whoever he pleases at knife-point.

The curtain opens. Enter stage left Buta on his way to the Technical Training Center to get some furniture polish. He meets Daku and Chita. The two of them have just attempted to rob the seminary clerk when they spot Buta. They search him for money, don't find any, and coerce him into joining their next enterprise.

The target for the three vandals is Rehmat, Ken's gardener. He is seized by both Buta and Chita. Buta claps a hand across the victim's mouth while Chita removes 20 rupees from Rehmat's pocket. Daku flourishes his knife an inch from the terrified gardener's stomach. The curtain closes.

As the curtain reopens, Ken is trying to calm Rehmat and make sense out of what his agitated gardener it trying to tell him. Ken requests immediate action from the local police station. There is. Within an hour Buta is being marched off to the lockup while Daku and Chita have vanished.

Events now seem to take place as though the stage has mysteriously become inverted and everyone has been trapped inside the action of some zany comedy.

Ken and Marie are having lunch with their niece, Valerie. Rakho rushes in from stage right. She sits on the floor, wailing loudly, and bursts into tears. She is served tea, which she passes on to an unknown woman who has entered from stage left and is attempting to comfort her. Ken, ever the coward, excuses himself lamely by saying, "When you remove the honey-pot the flies leave." He walks over to inspect the housing colony. Rakho is certain the police are beating Buta to death and, to hasten some action, cries louder. She's eventually persuaded to go to the police station to see for herself.

Intermission

Rakho, with a bundle of chapatis and a bemused uncle, comes to the kitchen during supper to ask if she can take Buta some food. As she leaves, a loaded police jeep comes to the front. Five men get out—a police captain resembling Kojak, a police lieutenant, a plainclothes man who looks like Fu Manchu, a policeman scribe, and the luckless Buta looking for an opportunity to do some effective crying.

Valerie serves tea.

The scribe borrows some paper and poises his pen to write. Events soon overtake his ability to process and record quickly enough. The victimized gardener is called and sits on the floor to give his testimony. Buta tries to ask for forgiveness. The captain emphasizes that this is a very serious case. Buta whimpers. The captain reads the applicable sections of the penal code. Buta whimpers a little louder. Inayat comes in and thumps Buta who whimpers louder still.

What does Mr. Old want? Mr. Old wants Daku brought under control. He is terrifying everybody. Very easy. Not to worry. He will be proclaimed a public offender. Why has Mr. Old copied the complaint to the Superintendent of Police? This is very embarrassing for the captain. Ken apologizes profusely.

"One little matter. Who are the witnesses?" The gardener himself of course. "Very good. And the other witnesses?" "There are no others." "What? There must be!" "No, there are no others." "There must be. Doesn't Mr. Old realize that the judicial system, based on that of his own country, requires at least two witnesses?" Well, they will have to manufacture one; it will only be a detail. Ken protests. "Is there any doubt about what has happened?" No, Buta admits it. "Well then, it's the duty of the police to prevent a miscarriage of justice." The cook, hovering near the door, is spotted. Now there is a likely witness, he'll do. Ken protests more strongly. "Let the case fail, there will be no false witnesses."

The captain stands up and removes his belt. He must have done this before for none of the expected consequences follow. He rubs his bare tummy. "What does Mr. Old think the Russians are going to do when they finish off Afghanistan?"

The scribe is wondering what he should write down.

Valerie serves more tea.

Rani, a bewildered little 16-year-old, appears on the verandah to tell Momma and Poppa Old she's back from Sialkot. "I don't know who it is I'm to marry or when it is to be. No one has told me."

Ken suggests, "Don't register the case until Sunday afternoon to permit Buta to become engaged, or married, or divorced." By this time no one is very sure what's going on. "Yes, this is possible. Buta will be allowed to search for Chita in the hostels." He's warned, "Don't tell him what is going on. Just tell him that all is forgiven." Buta departs. Buta returns. No Chita.

The lieutenant leans over and whispers to the captain, "We'd better go. We've been here two hours. I'm beginning to like what the respected Mr. Old has been saying about lying being the work of the Devil. If we stay here any longer, I'll become a Christian."

A new face appears at the door, Emmanuel. He brings a message, "The Principal of the seminary is coming."

The Principal, the seminary clerk, and two students appear and stand with Emmanuel. Chita and Daku have held up the clerk even before they robbed the gardener. "Although I withdrew 20 thousand rupees from the bank, it had all been dispersed before they tried to rob me. All that was left worth taking was my wristwatch. They took that."

Aha, now witnesses begin to line themselves up. "Did Wilson, one of the students, see it?" "Yes, Wilson saw what happened." The police captain refits his belt. Solutions are beginning to emerge. "We'll let it all be sorted out tomorrow at the seminary during supper."

The scribe writes the date and folds the paper carefully.

Inayat leaves for his night watchman duties, giving Buta a parting thump for spoiling a beautiful weekend.

Exit all, at intervals, animated.

Inayat has a Brilliant Idea

The wedding party has arrived from Wah. On no account must they know of Buta's brush with the law. The mysterious exits and entrances designed to keep them in the dark become increasingly confusing. Ken arranges another day's delay in registering the case against Buta to allow them to leave, but they don't.

Inayat has contingency plans for this situation should it deteriorate further. He has another bridegroom lined up for Rani and he juggles the two bridegrooms so that they will both be available at short notice when the weddings eventually get under way. However, he insists he will not permit Rani to be married before Buta. This produces total chaos and weeping and shouting.

Inayat needs to talk to Ken. It's extremely urgent. Ken has trouble understanding what Inayat is talking about. The faster Inayat speaks, the more incoherent he becomes. "I want a letter to the woman missionary in Sialkot." "Why?" Eventually Inayat reveals, "The missionary teacher has promised to find a wife for me if Mr. Old will give a note of approval." My goodness, a triple wedding?

Either Ken doesn't write a letter of approval or the teacher has no success in finding a wife for Inayat. Only the double wedding for Rani and Buta takes place. Now, history is repeating itself. Another double wedding!

Let us start somewhere at the beginning of the circle, wherever a circle begins.

Rani seems to be happily married. Buta's pretty little wife is a shrew. Both live in the north about 150 miles away. Peace in Gujranwala reigns like the monsoon. Inayat is wistful and never ceases plotting and scheming about getting someone to cook his chapatis. It hasn't worked out with Buta's wife.

He has found a role that suits him. He's the gardener. That's a wrong word. He knows nothing about gardening. He can't differentiate between weeds and flowers. What is the opposite of a green thumb? Maybe a black thumb. Every plant that he has anything to do with dies. They see him coming and they just wither and die. He hates grass with a vengeance. He begins swishing with his grass cutting sword outside the window at 4.30 a.m. No other gardener in all of Gujranwala has cropped as much grass to sell for fodder to the carriage drivers as Inayat.

All the time Inayat cuts grass, he's thinking. Thinking is the activity where Inayat most often gets into difficulty. Now he's thinking of his domestic arrangements. One of his slashes is halted in mid strike. Inayat has had an idea, a brilliant idea. The perfect solution to his problem.

He wants to shout. "Anwar! That's it. Why not Anwar? After all, he isn't good for anything else. Why not marry him to a chapati cooker who will cook, not only for her husband, but for her father-in-law who happens to live with them? Brilliant!" Inayat's mind is chewing on his first chapati as he begins to work on the details. 'This should be no more difficult than milking a buffalo. There will be one minor problem to get around, but for a man as resourceful as I am, only a hiccup.' Anwar is already married. His wife, like Inayat's own wife, has given up the unequal struggle and has run off with another man, and they now have a child.

Inayat's thoughts hardly pause over this insignificant detail. They're racing far ahead to the post-marriage situation. 'It's essential that, having brought about this desirable union, I will have to secure myself as a primary beneficiary of the young bride's superb cooking. They will need a home. They must share my home. As a father, it's my duty to share my humble home with my son. Mr. Old won't permit married children of employees to share their quarters. No problem.'

One morning Anwar, a slow-witted 30-year-old with hardly a thought in his head, appears for work at the pre-casting yard. Help may be needed, but Anwar is enough to make anyone pause. Even the simplest task needs some mental application. Ken already has two mentally deficient employees, and even they are astonished that Mr. Old would employ Anwar. Pity, sympathy, and kindness are well and good. But Anwar! Somewhere, even compassion needs to draw a line.

Inayat is delighted. "I'm almost there. Anwar is now an employee. Is he not then entitled to share his father's dwelling?" But of course.

The combined earnings of Inayat and Anwar, along with the income from grass, replenish the savings depleted by paying off the police to keep Buta out of jail. There's now almost enough for a wedding. Now an even brighter idea strikes Inayat. The ideas are coming fast and furious. 'Why not marry off Parveen at the same time and save the cost of a second wedding?'

Parveen has failed everything in school it is possible to fail. Marie won't let her come home for the summer holidays. There's no place in this boys' school suitable for her to stay. She stays at boarding school in Sialkot, like her sister Rani until a marriage can be arranged for her.

Ken tells Inayat, "No! Parveen is too young to be a bride. She's only 15." Inayat lies, "She is nearly 20. She will soon be too old for marriage." Ken brings a letter from Father Francis saying Parveen is 16 and her younger brother Kala is 14. Father Francis keeps well in the background. Parveen may be one of his flock, but the Catholic Church will probably survive even if that particular sheep, and all the family, should stray. Inayat now appears to have become a Protestant. To prove this, he asks Ken to deposit his rupee into the offering plate every Sunday. He's finding Padri William more pliable than Father Francis in the matter of Anwar's previous marriage.

Ken reluctantly says, "Alright. Parveen can get married, but not Anwar— he's already married." Inayat's anxiety is mounting. He says the respected Padre will marry Anwar anyway.

Inayat reports on his progress. He lets slip remarks about a beautiful muj—a water buffalo. How can a buffalo be considered beautiful except by another buffalo? Inayat is seeing superlative beauty in at least one of them. There's a beautiful muj in a nearby village that will become part of the dowry for the next marriageable daughter. The buffalo will be worth at least five thousand rupees. Kaki is young and beautiful, but not as beautiful as her dowry.

Inayat is gleeful. The grass cutting sword arm never tires. And here, wait for it, is the clincher! Kaki has a brother— young, handsome and virile—who will marry Parveen. "Isn't life wonderful? God is so good. What day shall be set for the double wedding? Next Friday?? He asks Ken, "Will you let me have a thousand rupees to buy a dowry for Parveen and presents for the buffalo's mistress, Kaki, my future daughter-in-law?"

Ken checks with Padri William. A slight obstacle emerges. The respected Padri will only marry Anwar if Anwar obtains a bill of divorce. Inayat reflects and rises to the occasion. He pays the doddering old storekeeper and the hostels sweeper to go secretly to the village where Anwar's wife lives in her new found bliss. They bring back a statement, in flowing Arabic script, on legal stamped paper. It's signed by the Muslim priest of the village mosque. It's a bill of divorce. What a coup! Inayat is on top of the world.

Now he must hurry if the wedding is still to be on Friday. Ken studies the content of the paper carefully. It declares that Anwar says his wife has left him for another man. Not good enough, Inayat.

Inayat thinks fast. The buffalo is almost within his grasp. Under no circumstances must the muj be lost. The alternative is Kala. She will substitute for Anwar. Ken says, "No. Kala is too young."

Ken appeals to Padri William to help Anwar get a divorce. It will cost 500 rupees. Ken suggests, "Inayat, you should also try to get a divorce at the same time."

This is a new line of thought for Inayat. He likes it. A chapati cooker of his own that he doesn't have to share with anyone! Inayat says, "The lawyer's clerk has agreed to do my divorce for nothing since I'm a poor man." The 500 rupees have been paid. There is much coming and going to the courts. The respected Padri is almost full-time on the job.

One day Padri William and a local legal go-between arrive. The divorce is done. The papers are valid. Eureka! The charge for success will be 100 rupees more. Ken gives Inayat the 100 rupees. Inayat goes to plead he's a poor man. They settle for 80.

Now the wind is set for fair sailing. The arrangements can go ahead without problems. They will spend two days doing the weddings, first Parveen's and then the buffalo a day later with Anwar and Kaki in attendance. Inayat, in his imagination, smooths the glistening black hide of his new love and hears the bidding rising—six thousand, six-and-a-half, seven thousand...

He asks Ken whether Thursday the 23rd and Friday the 24th will be auspicious days. Ken, cunning rascal that he is, concurs wholeheartedly. He has a court hearing in Lahore on the 23rd and committee meetings there the following day.

Members of Inayat's family begin to converge on Gujranwala. Rani comes and Buta and his wife. Buta is irate. He wants to marry Parveen to his wife's brother. He says, "Kaki's brother is an old man." Ken says, "Hold up the wedding. No old man for Parveen." Kaki's brother delivers the rice for the wedding feast. He's a young tractor driver and quite handsome. Inayat is growing nervous. Buta is going to spoil all the plans he's been making. He comes running to Marie. "Buta has gone off to Sialkot to kidnap Parveen and take her to Rawalpindi to marry his brother-in-law." Marie writes notes and Inayat is off to Sialkot lickety split.

Kaki's father is showing great affection for Ken and Marie. Slowly it emerges that Inayat has explained that, although Anwar and Parveen may legally be his progeny, spiritually and in every other way they belong to the Olds who are the true father and mother. This is comforting to Kaki's father. Although he wishes no disrespect to Inayat, if he had to make choices... well, there's no question. Inayat polishes this apple assiduously. "I am no more than a mere mirage in the existence of Anwar and Parveen. The Olds are everything." Marie, more than Ken, who is side-stepping rapidly, is inevitably drawn, against her will, into the vortex of a double Punjabi wedding.

The wedding gifts are brought for inspection—brightly colored cloths, rich velvets, and traditional Pakistani suits. Inayat has spared no expense he could not avoid. Earrings of gold. Kaki's father has said, "No earrings, no wedding." Ah well, there's always the buffalo.

The first wedding day dawns.

Ken, as Inayat's banker, hands Colin a checkbook with a blank, signed check. He admonishes Colin, "Do right by Inayat." And, sly fox that he is, Ken catches a bus to the sanctuary of the Lahore law courts. Colin sees his father leave with a tinge of trepidation. He's never been major-domo at an Eastern wedding before. He has, however, little time for reflection. Crises begin to enliven his day almost immediately.

Inayat has made a big mistake in inviting the teachers, but not the men at the yard that he and Anwar work with. This has turned his friends into enemies. He has also assumed that the rice delivered by Parveen's husband-to-be is all that will be needed for the wedding feast. Frantic activity develops. The wedding feast is at two. By ten o'clock they have firewood. By eleven o'clock they have cooking fat and meat. By 12:00 there is reconciliation with Inayat's fellow workers. The barber has his large cooking pots steaming away—three of plain rice, one of curry, and one of sweet rice. Parveen weeps uncontrollably, even more than a young bride should. The wedding and the feast pass in a blur. No one objects to the nuptials. Rita, Parveen's youngest sister, accompanies the bride to her new home. Inayat is all smiles. Colin settles with the barber, totally exhausted financially and physically.

Now for tomorrow and the buffalo. Inayat's joy is almost complete. Soon it will be overflowing.

Friday dawns bright and fair—until Inayat sees Ken once again preparing to leave for Lahore. "Who will drive the wedding van?" Ken smugly whispers a word into Inayat's ear and is off, full of regrets at deserting Marie.

Marie knows she shouldn't agree. She doesn't even know where it is that Inayat needs to go. He assures her, "It's only a little way, dear lady." He doesn't tell her that it is across the canal, or that the canal roads are closed with barriers, or that the tractors using the roads have so rutted them that you could lose a buffalo in the ruts. Nights later, in nightmares of desperate exertion, she is still wrestling the van in and out of potholes.

The second wedding too is completed. Poor Kaki becomes part of the Inayat menagerie. She and Anwar and Padri William, much delayed for his next wedding, come back with Marie. Had Inayat had his way, the buffalo would have traveled in the rear of the van and the rest would have walked. That way Marie wouldn't have had to remove the roof-rack to get under the canal barrier.

The bride shows her mettle. She knows her own family. Fine girl. Good beginning. She isn't leaving home unless her buffalo goes first. She has brought her up from a calf. Wherever Kaki goes the muj is sure to go, and go first. Inayat's approval of his daughter-in-law knows no bounds. He himself walks the buffalo home, arriving long after dark with the moon high in the sky.

All the long way he has been thinking. 'As a father I have done well by my two children. Conjugal bliss at last. How good to see Parveen and Anwar married to such fine partners. And such fine furniture as a dowry. Now I will have the reward of parenthood at last—chapatis and those great black / white eyes of the muj looking up at me. What more could a man ask for? Yes, God is good indeed.'

Scholarships Needed

K en and Marie have recently moved to Gujranwala which
is a city of dull flatness, dirty streets, dust-laden air, and
dust-coated trees. The main street is forever in traffic

chaos—jostling horse drawn taxi-carts and buffalo drays—and continual unfilled excavations for sewers and water mains. The railway gates are shut more than open, and the bazaar is a tangled congestion of shops with no recognizable pattern.

Yet for them, Guj has become more than that. It's a warm Christian community welcoming strangers like themselves, creating ripples in the water from the impact of a single drop of kindness. The colorful church congregation, to drums and the musical reed organ, sing the memorized couplets of the psalms with vigor and joy.

The Christian Technical Training Center is more than a school. It is also a place of hope. Those boys come from poverty such as we can never imagine—where from birth to death the natural hopes men thrive on are bruised, broken, and buried under burdens of debt and discouragement. Do they dare hope for a better life? As soon as the boys graduate, most of them earn at least double what their parents make. That means $20 a month instead of $10.

Ken is a man who has strong feelings about injustice. He can see the potential in every life, and wants to see that potential achieved. Children in the surrounding villages are being denied an education for the lack of a few small coins. Just four thin dimes a day is all that is needed. But the families are so poor that even with great sacrifice, the most they can manage is a single rupee—12 US cents or 8 English pence. And that represents one-third of their income. In America 12 cents is almost throwaway change.

The challenges for the school are many. Last spring, there were 80 trainees enrolled. Now there are 112 and by September Ken anticipates 120 trainees. Last week Ken was going through the boys' applications for reduced fees. The cost of training a boy is about 100 rupees a month or $12. Such a sum destroys the hopes of many for schooling. The obvious answer is to provide scholarships. The village boys are given forms to fill out. Ken reads through the applications. "My father earns 40 rupees a month and works as a peasant. There are nine of us children."

Another states, "My mother and father are dead. My brother works in the fields, but he has his own family and there are four more younger than me." These are the kinds of situations from which all the boys come. Tea is five rupees a pound and sugar almost a rupee. Even so, every boy is paying something towards his training. They can afford less than one rupee a day for food. They have lentils and bread for lunch, something a little better in the evening, leftovers and bread for breakfast, and only water to drink. There are *no* complaints. They thank God for giving them so much.

With the increasing enrollment, the need for scholarships is great. Ken's first appeal for help led to 24 boys receiving assistance for their schooling. Those sponsors have never made a more productive investment. The boys are being provided with hope of a better life than their parents. And they are so anxious to learn. Not many boys would ask for *more* mathematics, *more* theory, *more* practical work.

Now Ken makes a second request asking the church congregations, or youth or women's or men's groups, to consider under-girding a scholarship at $12 per month. He has used most of funds in the limited scholarship fund to sustain current scholarships, so the need is urgent. He assures them that every cent given will go into enriching an underprivileged Christian boy's life. Normally direct appeals for specific needs are discouraged, but because of its urgency, this appeal meets with no objections from the Mission in New York.

No less a challenge than finding scholarships is to use the time the young men are on campus wisely—helping them dare to dream of something beyond the plough and the brush. Ken seeks to give them a richer Christian experience, guiding them into unselfish decisions for the right reasons. He wants them to realize that being a Christian is a privilege rather than a burden, and that it carries responsibility for right living and right action.

The classrooms haven't been so full for many years. The Pakistani staff is giving loyal and enthusiastic service. There is little time to train the staff to take on full administrative responsibilities. Expatriate staff from England and Holland work alongside, but not in place of local staff. He hopes for additional volunteer staff from California, Ireland, and Germany.

Ken appreciates God's beautiful creation. Where they live in Gujranwala, the poinsettias are blazing red and tall behind the chrysanthemums in their sunlit garden. In December, their climate is similar to California, but without its smog or industrial haze. The winter rains are late, the skies are clear and Orion and the Pleiades lift over the horizon with startling clarity.

In his Christmas letter to friends and sponsors, he asks them to pray. "We need wisdom in these days of rapid change. We must see needs and be sensitive to rising aspirations. We need to 'ask and keep on asking, knock and keep on knocking' until the vision for this place can be realized. May God make this New Year rich for you beyond your expectation in the revelation of Himself incarnate in a carpenter's son. Paul writes of his hope, 'that ye may know Him'—what lovelier prayer than this for us to hold on to all year?"

God's Provision

We can approach God with confidence for this reason:
if we make requests which accord with His will,
He listens to us and if we know that our requests are heard,
we know also that the things we ask for are ours.

I John 5:14-15 NEB

K en is extremely grateful for any help he receives for his
boys. He considers each of them to be like a son. He is
very aware of God's wonderful provision. He and Marie
learned the truth of this when they worked in an orphanage in
Karachi fourteen years ago. They found that a prayer was better
than a bank balance. You can't overdraw on Him who said, "The
cattle on a thousand hills are mine."

Ken anticipated that 1971 would be a thrilling one. He
envisioned God providing for the needs of an unusual school with
few resources, but great reasons for being and serving. During
the elections, when all other schools, colleges, and technical
training centers closed, the Christian Technical Training Center
remained open.

Because he is confident that God has cattle on a thousand
hills, not just on one or two knolls, he isn't afraid to dream, and
dream big. He believes what the dusty old tribal leaders told
all Israel, "Not one promise that the Lord hath made hath
ever failed." Ken never thought that he could find joy in being

a beggar acting as an intercessor between those who need and those who love. But the task is easy when it's 'to strengthen the weak knees and lift up the hearts that faint'. Now his heart has already been lifted up this year! This down-to-earth, rather dull civil engineer, has often been moved near to tears as a need has no sooner appeared than it has been covered by a gift set in motion by God even before he was aware of the need. For instance—his boys have a very limited knowledge of English and have great difficulty in reading their textbooks. He wonders, 'How might we help them overcome this hurdle?' Then just last Friday, he heard that Forman Christian College in Lahore is willing to run a six-week intensive course in basic English this summer during the regular college vacation. It will cost about $16 per trainee. Phew! He wants to send 45 or 50 boys and it will cost $720 - $800! The following day a letter comes from a Church in San Mateo, California—'We are sending you our Christmas for Christ offering—approximately $720.' Ken immediately thinks of Psalm 81—'Open your mouth wide and I will fill it.'

Now contributions pour in from a wide range of donors. These include not only individuals such as other missionaries, but church congregations, Sunday School classes, and special offerings. Ken knows that most of these contributions come from those who would not be considered wealthy. Still, they have undertaken to help some of his kids out of the soil up a little nearer to the stars. Through them, God sent $4,836.25. That's enough for four months of education for a whole school! Pledges are made to provide scholarships, not only for one year, but on a continuing basis. Again, God's word leaps into Ken's mind. 'Let your hearts overflow with thankfulness. Colossians 2:7.'

Several days ago he wrote to groups in Germany, Holland, and the U.S. asking if they would help get a Leadership Development Program underway. He hopes that all the administration of this Center can be Pakistani within five years. This program is unlikely to bear much fruit for several years—and the first year alone needs $3,250! Phew, again! A Mission in New York indicates that, although they are in great financial difficulty, they are increasing their grant of help for the next three years by

$5,000 a year!

He also needs $730,000 to set the Center on a secure basis— about $410,000 for buildings and equipment, $300,000 in an endowment to make sure 250 poor boys can be trained in market place skills, and $20,000 for leadership development. Phew once again! But Ephesians 1:19 is an encouragement. 'How vast are the resources of His power open to us who trust in Him'.

A letter from a Dutch Church tells him they anticipate providing one fifth of the need if other partners will do the same. Does Ken doubt it? Of course not. He knows that the arms of the body of Christ reach around and join hands on the other side of the globe.

Ken's habit of reading his Bible daily without fail allows him to see everything that happens in terms of God's perfect timing. His absolute, unwavering trust in God helps him appreciate the abundant blessings showered down on him. It is also the reason he can maintain perfect peace. He has the assurance that God is always in control whatever the circumstance. This faith in God sustains him through many difficult times.

> No wonder we do not lose heart! Though our outward humanity is in decay, yet day by day we are inwardly renewed. Our troubles are slight and short- lived; and their outcome an eternal glory which outweighs them far. Meanwhile, our eyes are fixed, not on the things that are seen, but on the things that are unseen: for what is seen passes away; what is unseen is eternal."
>
> 2 Corinthians 4:16-18, NEB

Some of Ken's faithful supporters continue to fund scholarships long after he retires.

Anonymous Letter

Not everyone is happy for Ken to be at CTTC. A letter sent to the leaders of the Christian community maligns Ken's character. When he's given a copy, he is deeply hurt by the myriad of false accusations. But he maintains his composure. If this letter wasn't so deriding, it would be humorous. He has lived in Pakistan long enough that he is familiar with the tactics being employed. The writer attempts to secure his credentials by claiming to be a Christian, but what follows lacks any evidence of Christian love. The first paragraph does contain some actual historic facts, but everything after Ken's marriage to Marie is pure fabrication.

March 1972

Dear Sirs,

Greetings in the most precious name of our Saviour Lord Jesus Christ.

We are compelled by the circumstances to let you know the clear picture of the activities of Mr. K.G. Old, a missionary of the United Presbyterian Church at Christian Technical Training Center, Gujranwala, Pakistan. He is basically a building contractor, came to this land before Partition and independence through some English construction establishment until he married the widow of

Rev MacDonald, an American missionary. He managed to join Church World Services through her with no vision, dedication, or ordination.

We are sorry to say that he represents the British East India Company more than to represent Jesus through his life and acts. He indulges himself in the court cases by playing with the sentiments of the poor Pakistani Christians. He is proud of his intelligence and advocacy. The present situation of Christian Technical Training Center is a living testimony to his deeds. He is involved in court cases—i.e. before Labour Courts and High Court—against many CTTC employees to whom he has kicked out without cause. They could not assist his ambitions to loot and cheat a Christian Institution. He is wasting the donated funds to avoid the legal consequences.

He has been proved a culprit in the Court of Law in the petition moved against him by the Government of Punjab, Labour Department as he has locked out the Commercial Wing of CTTC which was not only a source to earn bread for many employees and to share the financial load of CTTC Training activities, but was also a practical opportunity to trainees. The reason stated by him is that he has been directed by the U.P. Commission and other donating bodies to do so.

There is also accusation against him by the Government of Pakistan, Customs Authorities, as he has illegally sold a vehicle which was imported through Church World Service without Custom duty, which was not to be sold or exchanged. He is still playing with the law by illegal sale of Custom free machinery and ruining the future of Christian institutions and missionaries in

Pakistan.

The majority of CTTC present Board of Directors are Mr. Old's self-appointed personal friends who appreciate his activities instead of distinguishing his illegal and wrong policies.

We request you to remove Mr. K.G. Old and his deputy Mr. B. Kuyvenhoven immediately from their present position to save this Christian Center. Evidences can be provided to these facts on your official contact with us.

God Bless you richly, Yours sincerely in Christ.

The letter is not signed.

Knowing the accusations are completely false, Ken has no need to defend himself.

A Home in England

K en and Marie and the boys spend two and half months in England in late '72, early '73. They are looking for a home base since Tim and Colin will need to return to England for further education after they graduate from Murree. They are clearly led to a dilapidated 15th century farmhouse near Dover, close by the old Roman road into Canterbury. Ken can envision the perfectly charming dwelling rising like a phoenix out of rubble. Marie can only see the obvious— an abandoned house with a gaping hole in the roof, and a door hanging by one hinge flapping in the wind. All the windows in the sun-porch and most in the house are broken.

The interior is questionable. The two staircases to the second floor are almost unusable. There is empty space where steps should be. The floor above the water cellar is missing some boards caused by a piano crashing through it. It's just impossible.

The other buildings are even worse. No roof on the cattle shed—or is it a chicken house? Perhaps even a pig sty. The barn is open to the elements, and the corrugated roof over the wagon and carriage shed is corroded with rust.

Ken enlists the aid of his brother to convince Marie the chaos can indeed be reduced and reformed into habitable accommodations. The confirmation for Ken is the lead verse in Daily Light for February 7th. That day, after eating breakfast and before beginning their journey to ask about purchasing the property, Marie reads: "When thou hast eaten and art full . . . thou shalt bless the LORD thy God for the good land which he hath given thee." Ken's response is, "He means for us to have it!" Marie has to agree when the owner asks for less than what they had determined in advance they would be willing to pay.

Located on the edge of a Common where no construction can ever take place, the nearest neighbors are half-a-mile away and happen to be friends who were former missionaries in Pakistan. Wheat fields surround three sides of the land. The uncultivated area beyond the farmhouse is home to pheasants and partridges. It is lovely countryside with rolling downs and hawthorn trees that burst into full bloom in May. Blackberries and elderberries grow profusely along the lane up to the gate.

The property, which includes the farmhouse, an open air barn, stables, and the walls of an animal enclosure, has been badly neglected and vandalized. Ken will keep the farmhouse and stables and one field. The remaining land and buildings will go to his brother as payment for renovation. Because some of the structures at Gibbins Brook Farm date back as far as 1460, they are considered 'listed' buildings. Historic buildings are precious and finite assets, powerful reminders of the work and way of life of earlier generations. The exterior can be repaired, but must retain its original architectural appearance.

Ken provides drawings of the layout for the interior. There will be six bedrooms and three bathrooms upstairs. The ground floor will make use of the original long room for a combination dining / living room. A large kitchen, a small pantry, a bathroom off the entry way, and a smaller informal living room complete the interior. For the next 15 months, while Ken works in Pakistan, his brother is racing to complete the necessary repairs and modifications. The home must be ready for Marie and the boys by the summer of 1974. Aerogrammes wing from Pakistan to England and back several times a week.

Monday, July 16th, 1973

Dear Tonio,

Your letters, two of them, have just come and I will catch the post today to get this reply back to you to.

Yesterday I came back from visiting Marie and the boys in Murree. She has a gastric ulcer, but was much better and brighter in herself. The boys are well, busy with basketball, school lessons, and various other activities related to a normal school life. We anticipate that at least Marie and the two boys will return to the UK next summer to put in some work on the house and the gardens. In addition, they will arrange whatever further schooling is necessary. It appears Colin would be better off finishing out here next year and then go on to study architecture. He likes the idea. Even when Marie and I come back to Pakistan, he may well continue to live at Sellindge and study either at Ashford or Canterbury.

Now, about the house.

I did the various amendments to the drawings several weeks ago, but I have had the draftsmen very busy on buildings I have going up here which cost about $45,000.

I am glad you are doing up the stables. That makes good sense. I see it eventually as a home for somebody. Do you think the barn will be approved for use as a dwelling for yourself?

It is interesting that the estate agent came down. It makes me think about whether I would sell it.

I had to pay about $300 interest to the bank. The use of money does cost money. Dad has offered to loan me some money to avoid the heavy bank interest rate, but I am not sure that would be wise.

I have done a plan of the access road and paths. Marie will decide where to plant trees. We are thinking mainly of fruit and flowering trees like cherries.

What is the soil like? I am assuming it is chalky and will plan to dispose of the waste from the septic tank in herringbone surface drains.

I have agreed to the suggestion of the planners about the windows, but Marie isn't too happy about losing some of them.

Keep accounts of everything we should pay you for when we have money. Where are you getting water from?

I have no trouble at all from law cases these days, although I got a summons last week for another case in Sialkot. The other cases are in the High Court, which has ordered that proceedings in the lower courts be stayed until they make a decision.

I'll be sending drawings soon.

Love to all of you, Ken

The council doesn't approve plans for converting the barn into a dwelling so Ken gives his brother the stables and additional land, keeping only the farmhouse and one third of the property for himself.

While one brother is busy in Sellindge, the other is overwhelmed in Pakistan. Ken doesn't write again until October.

October 1st, 1973

Dear Tonio,

I haven't been able to write many letters recently since I have been involved in flood relief committees. I have designed a pre-fabricated concrete house for flood housing. I am sitting in the Finance Ministry in Islamabad waiting to see the Finance Minister. There is every likelihood it will be produced in the scores of thousands.

We have been wondering what has been happening at GBF —have you run into any building snags? We are interested in all your details.

We are still working on getting the farm paid for— a check for nearly $400 was stolen in the mail and cashed in Germany so we are fighting that.

We took Tim to the hospital for x-rays of his scoliosis on Saturday. He was advised to carry on as usual. Present plans are for Marie and the boys to go to GBF in June. I may do so also although that will depend on the situation here.

Love to you all, Ken

The time for moving to England draws near when Ken writes to his parents on the 25th of May, 1974.

Dear Mum and Dad,

We are so glad about the way God is working in Timmy's life. He has been blessed to learn faith 'like a child' without having to dot all the 'i's and cross all the 't's.' Now we will be able to rest in God's providing for him. We are so grateful to you for taking Tim into your hearts.

Marie has gone to Murree for the 'special' service for the kids leaving school. She will come back tomorrow and we'll go back on Wednesday for Colin's graduation on Thursday. He'll come down for the weekend and then return to take his series of O-level exams which end on June 17th. Early on the 20th he and Marie leave for London. Tell Tonio if he can get one toilet working by the time Marie gets there this will be good.

Recently, I have been involved in a housing solution for 100 refugee families from Bangladesh. My house building yard is being transferred to Lahore by June 15th so that will be one burden unloaded.

Thanks Dad for all your effort at Sellindge. I hope that house will be a joy to us all. Ken

Marie embarks on a new life; a life of building a home in her husband's country, caring, cooking, and chauffeuring her two tall sons. The only services to the farm are electricity and the postal delivery. The only heat comes from the fireplace in the long room. Heat for the upstairs must be provided by electric heaters which are expensive to run.

When Ken comes on short visits, he and Marie have fun hunting second hand furniture in auctions and sale rooms. Colin and Tim enjoy having a home they don't have to leave nine months each year for boarding school. Both boys, now 17, are working. Colin is a craftsman at an engineering consulting firm in a lovely market town eight miles away. Tim works on a pig farm five miles towards Canterbury, enjoying the challenge and discipline of open air labor while he waits for the Lord's leading for his future.

Marie finds life without Ken difficult and looks forward to the time she can return to her beloved Pakistan. In the meantime, she plants Leyland Cypress trees as a wind-block just beyond the glassed-in sun-room and another row between the house yard and the back field. Two apple trees, a cherry tree, and a pear tree will eventually provide fruit. A large Hawthorne tree, known as a May tree for the time of year it blossoms, and a Holly tree provide both shade and beauty. Each birthday, anniversary, or other special occasion results in a new rose bush being planted. Soon the garden is blazing with colors of every shade and lovely bouquets brighten and scent the air inside.

Strangely Warmed

November 1974

Ken and Marie are on furlough and are due to return next August. However, Ken isn't taking advantage of it. He is staying for two-months now and will perhaps return in the spring.

During the summer in England, and now again in Gujranwala, he feels 'strangely warmed' by an assurance that the

Holy Spirit is moving, and moving with power. In both places, in ways he hasn't felt before, there is new awareness of the 'gifts'. And, with it, a bursting out of praise and joy. Old structures and forms are disappearing. The United Presbyterian church of Pakistan appears to be disintegrating under pressure. But lay people, often young people, are now leading.

At the school, it is a joy to Ken to see the graduates returning to the world they came from a year or so previously entirely different than when they came. They go out armed, not only with that bright and shining certificate that means so much, but also with self-assurance, self-respect, deepened faith, and an artisan skill. Allah Ditta, a simple country boy with a big smile, comes to give Ken salaams. Most of his brothers are still illiterate and work with their peasant father on the land. But an elderly missionary coached Allah to prepare him for CTTC. He finished top of his class and earned the prize for 'best try-er'. Now, making doors and windows, he earns $30 a month—three times as much as his father. Another graduate, Zafar Iqbal, also comes by. He is a poor Khokherke boy now earning the handsome salary of $45 per month as a draftsman in Lahore.

Ken's dream, when he came here four years ago was to have a full 100 trainees graduate each year. They will be close to that next year. The first phase of his development plan is nearly complete with more than 150 enrolled at present. The German Evangelical Church, donors of the buildings and equipment, will decide next spring whether the second phase of expansion to 250 boys should proceed.

The flood relief and low cost housing project has been transferred to Lahore and progresses well. The work is not only in physical areas, there is also a work of the Spirit. Everyone needs a constant deepening of faith, a constant proving of His faithfulness. There should be a hunger for more responsiveness in our own souls to His impulses, more awareness of His sustaining presence, more readiness to commit ourselves entirely.

The law cases that have plagued Ken have continued, awaiting a High Court decision on whether CTTC is a school or an industry.

Prime Minister Bhutto's government seems unchallenged. And Pakistan has deepening problems. There has been an appalling rise in the cost of basic food staples. The whole sub-continent faces immense food shortages. It is becoming increasingly difficult for Pakistani Christians to find work. An itinerant preacher convinced Afzal of need for Christ. Rejected by his father, he was ejected from his home. His wife returned to her family and divorced him. He sends Ken a letter from Lahore:

> Dear Uncle,
>
> I gave your letter about work to Mr. Wolf yesterday, but he denied me with lame excuses. Do pray for the problem for it has been going on for three months now. I am fearing it could be a reason created by Satan to spoil my testimony for Jesus Christ.
>
> Yours in His Love, Afzal

His search for work has been unsuccessful, but his deep commitment shines through in his gentle spirit and intensity of faith.

Another example of life-changing faith is that of an elderly Christian woman of Hindu background who recently died. She lived in nearby congested Khokherke. She was slight, frail, and devout. She regularly purchased portions of Scripture and distributed them in the bazar. She would rise at 2 a.m. to pray, read her Bible, and recite the 200 verses she had memorized. When she died, her husband came by to inform Ken and shared a note she had written:

> No true faith-winged prayer goes unanswered.
>
> Many a prayer that seems to us unanswered is really over answered. The very thing we ask, God does not grant because He is able to do something infinitely better for us.
>
> Thus, many times, our little prayers are really

over answered.

Christmas is a time of refreshing for Ken. It shines with glory in this world which is frequently drab and colorless. It sings compassion when the world is mute and it insists on being heard, though the world turns away. Its message is:

Peace on earth

Goodwill toward men.

His name shall be called Emmanuel

Which means

God with us.

A Bigger Dream

May 1st, 1978

When God becomes real to us, all sorts of eddies, whirls and ripples flow around us. We hear of so many wonderful things happening as the Holy Spirit moves with power among people. Things are happening in Gujranwala too. The Spirit *is* moving and lives are infused with a sense of expectancy.

A local women's Bible study, the United Bible Training Center begins meeting on Wednesdays. Started by Ken's neighbor, Jean Mullinger, they expect maybe a dozen women. Instead, 30 women come and the four nuns among them bring 30 of their girls so they can learn how to really study the Bible.

Camp Mubarak is located in Murree, 5,000 feet above the Punjab plains. For two successive weeks each spring and fall, 50 or so boys from CTTC are privileged to attend this 'Camp of Blessing' where they discover a personal relationship with Christ. Surprisingly, some of the applications for attending camp come from Muslim students wanting to be allowed to participate.

After the camp is over, one of the boys from CTTC asks Ken, "Why didn't I receive the Holy Spirit like James?" Ken suggests, "Why don't you ask God?" He took the suggestion to heart, and each afternoon, 10 or 15 boys go to the Chapel to seek God's blessing.

Walter Crowe, now retired in Michigan, recently revisited

his old home and met folks who remembered him as a boy. His father, here for more than 30 years, was the 'father' of CTTC and built the chapel 60 years ago. Each morning its capacity of 320 is overtaxed. Soon the chapel will need to enlarged.

Over 150 new boys, admitted less than a month ago, are now attending regular corporate worship. More than half these boys come from small clusters of Christian peasants and sweepers scattered throughout the country and to them regular worship is a new experience. Their singing is ragged, but sincere. This is where the heart of CTTC beats.

With 375 boys, CTTC now has 50 percent more boys than Ken planned for in 1971. Each year, more than 700 apply for admission. He has often seen God's abundance overflowing the far reaches of his daring hopes. Whenever Ken has been wrong in his planning, it has always been that he didn't see far enough, never that he saw too far. Our German donors of buildings and equipment have permitted the use of some unspent funds towards the cost of a seventh hostel unit of 50 beds. This will bring the capacity to 315.

Before the boys even graduate in March, Government factories offer jobs to the fitters, welders, machinists, and draftsmen. Not only did the students go, but also almost half of the instructors—13 of them. However, all the gaps were quickly filled by the graduates. Trades most in favor with the boys change over time. During the past seven years, they have moved from auto mechanic to machinist to welder to electrician, and now draftsman. This is an easy course to expand as it only requires additional drawing tables. The two years stay of these boys makes possible extended nurture in a Christian environment.

Ken is Secretary of the Society for Community Development. This society seeks to assist members of the Christian community to witness their faith in Jesus Christ through their lives and service. Vocational training is part of this. CTTC is reaching down into the lives of boys with less and less education and opportunity. However, even CTTC doesn't go far enough.

Ken has a dream for a new school, which will take more than

200 boys, one-half without any previous schooling. It would be a school for building trade artisans— brick masons, bar-benders, steel-fitters, plumbers, gas-fitters, painters, decorators, plasterers, and carpenters. In addition, there would be training for educated boys as building supervisors, site foremen, draftsmen, estimators, quality and cost surveyors. No such school exists in this country of 76 million people.

The plans are drawn. The total cost, including an endowment of $250,000, will be $935,000. The first $10 came a year ago from a foreign visitor. He was told, "We'll build a school with this." Now Ken has $1,338 in the bank *and* a dirt access road into the field where the school will be located.

A cashier, looking around wonderingly at the new CTTC that has risen before his eyes, says "Sir, for years we were all praying for this, but we didn't know what we were praying for. We couldn't even imagine it and now, all of a sudden, we can see what it was we were praying for. Isn't God wonderful?"

Ken is thanking God, not only for dreams, but for the fulfillment of dreams.

He has asked that, if possible, he be replaced as Principal of CTTC by the spring of 1979 so that he can give more attention to the building school and the low cost housing program that is linked with it.

He won't be able to get away, but Marie is going to England for Tim's wedding on June 10th. Cathy is a student nurse in his class. They will live in the farmhouse after their marriage. Colin, who hopes to revisit Pakistan this summer, would like to be a squash racquets professional. His parents would like him to complete his education first.

God gives them a surrogate son in Simon, a 19-year-old taking a year off before entering an English university. He is proving immensely helpful. Yesterday an Englishman turned up who is a draftsman and can play soccer. God will have a purpose here for him also.

$\mathcal{G}uidelines$

Ken and Marie host young adults from around the world who volunteer to spend a few weeks or an entire summer helping with some project. Often it is more work to define a project than the help derived, but undoubtedly the greatest value is for those who come and have life-changing experiences.

Although Pakistan is a modern country, some of the customs of the culture can seem quite outdated to youngsters accustomed to the freedoms of the West.

Ken sets down some guidelines for adjusting to a different culture. It is required reading for all volunteers as soon as they arrive, even before they are settled into their new lodgings.

Some Guidelines to Help You Adjust to a Different Culture

Since it is often difficult for young people from the West to adjust to an Eastern culture, we are offering the following guidelines to help make the transition a bit easier. We hope you will observe them and take them in the spirit in which they are offered.

1. The *only* social contacts for Pakistani girls are with other women. We should regulate our life styles in conformity with this. If we do so, we will not be an embarrassment to our

Pakistani colleagues, or to the Gospel in our own ministry, or in the ministry of others.

2. Girls must not go out or come back alone after dark. It is necessary for you to adjust your going out so that you are in before dark unless you have one of our expatriate young men escorting you.

   If there is some unavoidable circumstance which makes it impossible for you to get back before dark from journeys outside our own town, arrange to stay overnight and travel the next day. If you must do this, please try to phone the school and tell someone. If you get no answer from CTTC then try UBTC. Please have these phone numbers with you when you go out of town.

3. No men at all should be entertained in girls' houses. Consider your house out of bounds for Pakistani men. Our arrangement of all the expatriates eating together makes this difficult here, but when our young expatriate men are eating in the house, it should be in a room in full view of the outside and they should not stay in the house when meals are finished unless there is a married couple present or a senior person from UBTC or our own staff.

4. It is possible to be in the same company where there are Christian Pakistani boys if our Western boys are also there. However, be very careful of your behavior. It will be watched carefully by these young men and reported in the community with a few extra details. They will be judging you against the standard of demure behavior of Pakistani girls in male company.

5. There will be no meeting between girls and Muslim boys in groups or alone.

6. If young men come to see the boys when girls are present the boys must immediately take their friends somewhere else. No Muslim boys will be allowed in the eating arrangement at all. If the boys want to have Muslim guests for a meal, they should take them out to eat.

7. Western boys should be concerned for their sisters in Christ and avoid putting the girls into a difficult situation. Be alert to respond to it if it does happen.

8. If you want to go to the movies please do not do it in Gujranwala. Do it in Lahore, but always with a suitable escort. It is not good for Christian girls to be seen in the movie theater here.

9. In public, in the bazaar, walking on the roads, or riding public transportation, behave with decorum—no loud laughing or talking.

10. Swimming in the canals in mixed groups is absolutely not acceptable. Girls should only swim if there are no onlookers at all.

11. Men callers at the girls' house should be ignored if possible. If the cook is there, have him answer the door and send them away or refer them to the Olds. The Olds stand in the place of your parents while you are here and can be a useful buffer for you when necessary.

12. Do not go into the main Gujranwala bazaar alone—there should be at least two together at all times.

13. A chiffon scarf called a doppata is an essential part of female dress when out. Please keep your head covered when you are in the bazaar

or walking about the streets of Gujranwala. Lahore is different.

14. Boys should be neatly dressed as are their colleagues.

15. Don't go *anywhere* without telling someone where you are going.

16. When you leave Gujranwala for any other place, please tell either the Olds or Miss Mullinger where you are going and when you expect to be back. It is just practical wisdom. We never go without telling someone where we are going.

17. Immediately report any unpleasant incidents that occur.

18. Please attend the Urdu church services somewhere on Sundays. This makes you part of the Christian community you have come to serve. The community wants you to feel part of it and to worship with it. Don't isolate yourself. It doesn't matter that you don't understand Urdu. Worship involves fellowship.

19. The Tuesday evening prayer meeting is optional, but do please attend the Sunday evening fellowship meeting regularly unless you are out of town. It is the one time of the week to get together. We are each important to the others, and we need this spiritual fellowship. This meeting has been the missionary focal get-together for 125 years and it should have priority in your activities.

20. Weddings, engagements, bereavements are an important part of community life anywhere, but especially so here. Share in these occasions as much as possible.

21. Boys, be ready to change your plans to be an escort for the girls when they need this. Their lives are much more circumscribed by custom so you must cheerfully help them. Include them in your activities as much as possible.

22. It is quite true than many Pakistani boys, including Christians, have the impression from movies and videos that life in the West is one long party of drunkenness and sexual immorality. The free and easy behavior that occurs in the West, in relationships between the sexes, and a girl's general freedom, are seen in contrast with the restricted / protected lives of Pakistani young people. It can be interpreted as proof of our own moral standards. This is the last thing we want.

23. Strangely though, even after all these rules, it is possible to be very happy here.

We gratefully appreciate your cooperation and acceptance of these guidelines.

Reading through these stringent rules must have caused many of the girls to wonder what they had gotten themselves into. Being free and independent is a way of life not easily tossed away. It will take immense concentration every single day to consistently conform to the Pakistani culture. When girls gather together, they can't help but laugh and sometimes with loud shrieks. Keeping that under control will be difficult. Some girls may be flirtatious. That would be a big no-no. But Ken and Marie will steer the girls … and the boys as well … into proper eastern culture behavior. There will be a few awkward situations that Ken has to smooth over, but for the most part, all the volunteers are extremely conscientious and cooperative.

Seeing God

Ken has the ability to see events from God's perspective. He never accepts that things happen for no reason. He doesn't believe in coincidences. No matter what the circumstance is, Ken sees God's hand at work. He firmly believes the truth of scripture.

> Follow peace with all men, and holiness,
> without which no man shall see the Lord.
> Hebrews 12:14

How does one see God? Not with the eye, certainly, but we do see Him as His loving hand reaches out to His needy children. We see Him as He takes us beyond ourselves into situations where He is already present and waiting for our response. A loose, but perhaps permissible, paraphrase of this scripture might be 'A man living a holy life will see God in everything.'

Each day, from before dawn until he hits his nine p.m. deadline for bed, Ken sees his loving Father at work. He finds God in the rich vineyard He has created at CTTC and he sees Him moving him into fresher fields also. He reflects on some of them.

Seeing God in Pasrur—30 miles east of Gujranwala the Christian Home for poor children cares for 60 boys and girls until they reach teenage. Most have lost one parent. The children feel the Home is their real home and are clean, cared for, and well nourished. The boys tend to move on into CTTC when they are old enough. This Home is supported by Christians in West Germany and Berlin.

Ken visited on a Sunday, and preached in the local Pentecostal church. It is beautifully kept and cared for. The congregation, most of them children, sit on the floor. A woman plays the hand held drum. One disabled villager has come for healing. The service lasts two hours.

Seeing God in Chang—60 miles south of Gujranwala, wasteland at Chang is being cultivated under the guidance of farmers from Washington State and Colorado. In the various water courses are concrete structures to keep the water flow in check. These have been made at CTTC in the building research and development unit.

Seeing God in Taxila—160 miles north of Gujranwala, not far from the famous Mission hospital in Taxila is a heavy mechanical complex provided by China. It includes a forge and foundry. The Chinese technicians are hard-working and respected. Almost 100 CTTC graduates work in these two factories, and are well regarded for their practical ability.

Ken has done some development work on low cost buildings. The government asks him to be the architect for a high school adjacent to the factory. He accepts and is told "You are a missionary to Pakistan, but you are also a missionary *for* Pakistan. You have to sacrifice to help us. We will only give you a 1 percent fee."

Seeing God in Rawalpindi—137 miles north of Gujranwala, a man throws his Bible across the room. "That book has brought me nothing but trouble." He was initially thrilled and captivated by the freshness of this new book. But as the call for commitment grips him, the cost begins to bear more and more heavily on him. He has lost his family, friends, and business—it is just too much! So he tries Freud instead, but still, a voice in his head beats more insistent, "He that followeth after righteousness and mercy findeth life, righteousness, and honour." Proverbs 21:21 Back to that Bible again.

Seeing God in Gujranwala—Chapel at 7:00 on a cold morning. About 350 boys and 40 staff sit in pews and on benches. They strain to understand a happy, well-educated, young man talking in the guttural Urdu used in the north. He wears dark glasses. "I was robbed while on a pilgrimage. A Christian couple befriended me. When I left them, they gave me twice the amount that was stolen as a love gift to a stranger. I read their holy book to find out why they had done this. Later, I confided my new belief that had gripped me to my parents. They were appalled. One night I woke up with a shriek of pain. My mother laid a hot iron across my eyes. Many other trials followed. I was a radio announcer, but now I sell Scripture Union notes in a suburb of Islamabad to any who will buy."

Ken asks, "Do you have any sight left?"

The young man removes his glasses. Only the eyeless sockets remain.

What unquenchable power Christ has, when to follow Him in such circumstances can be so much joy! Ken does see Satan's struggle wherever God is working, but in life after life he sees victory also.

Seeing God in Murree—170 miles north from Gujranwala, each spring and fall 100 boys who have completed their first six months at CTTC go to the mountains for a week. The boys are challenged to commit their lives to Christ. Edison went to the second one in October. He and his companions determined that nothing was going to happen to *them!* For four days they were like a brick wall. Before 'lights out' a friend asked Edison to pray. "Who, me? OH NO, I'm going to have a smoke." Then a voice that only he heard knocked him back: "Edison, get on your knees and pray." He did. It is though heaven descended on the Murree hills. Forty of the boys are now taking confirmation classes each morning.

Ken loves this troubled country in which he lives and its people. He sees God at work in both its troubles and responses.

The Christian community at last realizes how urgently it must develop adequate religious nurture for its people. The boys from CTTC each have and use their own daily devotional scripture notes. Marie has a weekly time for prayer with her Pakistani women friends. Ken leads a weekly Bible study class, 'Christians and Conflict'. He also teaches it to the Seminary students.

So how *does* one see God? We see Him as faith in Jesus Christ transforms people and situations. We see Him as the Holy Spirit makes us aware of each other, as He moves among and between us. We see Him in hearing again Mary's submissive "Yes" and her boy's first startled cry.

A Sermon for the
Sunday after Easter

One spring Ken is in the hills at Murree Christian School over the Easter holiday. He is asked to give a sermon which he entitles, 'A Sermon for the Sunday after Easter.' When he prepares a sermon, he spends days composing it. It's always a long sermon—at least 30 minutes, sometimes longer. He feels if he's asked to preach, he should be given as much time as he likes. He captivates his audience and no one stirs or coughs the entire time. He has a unique way of phrasing things. He creates sentences that are not straightforward, but make you listen to the end to discover the point. His voice is deep and resonates with the love of God. He captivates his listeners: earning their trust and making them feel secure. Ken begins with a scripture reading from John 20:18–24.

> "Mary Magdalene came and told the disciples that she had seen the Lord, and that he had spoken these things unto her. Then, the same day at evening, being the first day of the week, when the doors were shut where the disciples were assembled for fear of the Jews, came Jesus and stood in the midst, and saith unto them, Peace be unto you. And when he had so said, he showed unto them his hands and his side. Then were the disciples glad, when they saw the Lord. Then said Jesus unto them again, Peace be unto you, as my Father hath sent me, even so send I you. And when he had said this, he breathed on them, and saith unto them, "Receive ye the Holy Ghost; Whose soever sins ye remit, they are remitted unto them; and whose soever sins ye retain, they are retained." But Thomas, one of the twelve, called Didymus, was not with them when Jesus came.

"It is the week after Easter, the hustle and bustle, the preparation and exhilaration, are over. What now?

"Have you ever wondered what might have been going on in Jerusalem a week after the event? Who were some of the principals involved in the Crucifixion? Who were some of the others—the people in the streets, the shopkeepers, the housewives, the donkey cart drivers. What were they making of what had just happened? We, with the hindsight of 19 1/2 centuries, know better than they what they should have been watching, but, blinded by their nearness, what *were* they thinking of it all?

"Let us allow our imagination to run wild for a bit.

"I want to look briefly at four people during that eighth day after the Passover Sabbath.

"Let me first recognize that the Feast, the Festival, had just ended. Passover was merely the first of the eight days of the feast of unleavened bread in the month of Nisan, lasting from the 14th to the 21st. That last night, marking the end of the gathering for another year, was also a celebration with special services at the Temple. The pilgrims that had crowded the Holy City had come from nearby and as far as the four corners of the Dispersion. They would remain camped in and around the city until it came time to disperse with daylight on the 22nd. Up to 200 thousand lambs were said to have been slaughtered in the Temple precincts prior to the Passover with much of Jewry sharing in the celebrations. No wonder the services of Judas had been needed to locate Jesus on that Thursday night. The crowds were everywhere.

"Let us recognize the important part that the High Priest, Caiaphas, is playing in keeping order. Colonial powers throughout history have tried to avoid having their troops tied down, keeping civil populations under control. They have always preferred to keep their troops strategically garrisoned in barracks, available to call into action when less reliable arrangements for civil management broke down. It would be up to the civil governor, the viceroy, the commissioner, the deputy commissioner, the proconsul, to sort out feasible arrangements by which the people would continue to be governed and, eventually, taxed. These arrangements were mixtures of carrot and stick. Favors, promotions, preferential treatment, education of children in Imperial Centers (providing useful hostages if necessary), invitations, honors, and gifts and grants of land were never far from the mailed fist within the velvet glove that all who participated in the game being played knew was present. Caiaphas, and Herod Antipas too, like many before and since, walk a knife edge. One slip and they are finished and they know it.

"Take Caiaphas now that it's all over. He heard of the raising of that man Lazarus at Bethany, so his willingness to have one man die that the nation shall be safe, has borne its planned fruit.

But what of the next day? Things were not yet under control. He had personally given the orders for the watch to be set over the tomb. It was to him that the captain of the watch and his men had come running as dawn was breaking. He was already up. He had been checking damage after the earthquake. The men were hardly coherent. The fools! Disregard the talk of angels. The essential thing was that the body was gone. It's just what he suspected might happen. He would sort out how it had been done later. He acted without delay.

"He sent for all the members of the Sanhedrin with an immediate call. They agreed with his proposals. 30 pieces of silver each to bribe the men on watch, and well worth it. A story was rehearsed before them and all have agreed. 'A band of Galileans came while they slept. Outnumbered, they daren't move. Then the tomb was empty.' The men were sent off to spread the news before other rumors got out.

"Then had come his visit to Pilate. A private meeting with no one else present except the interpreter. Pilate spoke no Aramaic and little Greek. Pilate questioned him hard and curiously. He wasn't satisfied. The High Priest had seen that. No matter. Their concern was common. There must be no rioting while the city was packed with pilgrims. Keep the lid on and the rumors down until the crowd had dispersed after the eighth day.

"Caiaphas sent for Lazarus. The man had come reluctantly, under escort, trembling and stammering. He told the story he had now told many times, the story that had started it all. Curse the man. He had been dead; why didn't he stay dead! He didn't know anything, he had died and then he was alive. He had no recollection of what had happened in-between. Caiaphas jabbed him with his staff a vicious thrust under the ribs as though he expected it to go right through. Unnerved, he had Lazarus committed to prison, as a danger to the peace, until the Festival was over.

"And a week later, Caiaphas was still trying to find out what happened. How had the Galileans done it? For the rumors were flying thick and fast. The ghost of Jesus had been seen, but not a ghost. Something different – and impossible. Something physical. And seen, not just by one or two, not just the Galileans who had hatched the conspiracy, but Judeans as well. Two were reported to have seen him, in broad daylight, on the coast road, miles from the city. There were things you could only put down to the wildness of rumor fire – a ghost can't eat even if you should happen to see it. Caiaphas had his informers all out. His power rested, and he survived, on the extent and reliability of his information service. Even the Romans had no idea how widespread that network was. The conversation at every meal in the palace, and the tower was reported back to the High Priest. His men, and women, were looking for, and listening to, every Galilean in the city. Nothing solid was coming in. The followers of Jesus had either fled or were in hiding.

"He had sent for Joseph and Nicodemus. Were they sure he had been dead? How did they know? They had been sure, certain sure. They knew the signs of death. Both of them were old men, and experienced, with reputations for integrity and truthfulness. Would they not have seen, even hoped for, any signs of life if there had been any? But there were none. The man they had buried was a dead man. They had no doubt about it. They had seen many dead. Then, was someone impersonating him? And, if so, who? And where was the body if that were so?

"What was it the man had said to him that morning? 'Hereafter shall ye see the Son of man sitting on the right hand of power and coming in the clouds of heaven.' Caiaphas needed explanations other than his own rumors and he wasn't getting them. He would heave a sigh of relief when the crowds had all dispersed.

"And Pilate—what of him? He had his informers too, not as extensive a network as Caiaphas who was on his own ground. But they were paid well and had proved reliable. Pilate, reflecting on his release of Barabas and his action against Jesus, had been uneasy even before the Crucifixion had taken place. He admitted to himself he had not done well. The man was innocent, of course, but what is a man to do? Justice is a mockery, only the naïve believe in it, and innocent people often get hurt. It wasn't the first time an innocent man had been sentenced to death. This was just one of those unfortunate cases.

"He didn't like Palestine; the religious undercurrents were beyond his understanding. Fanatics are not particularly susceptible to threats of force. He wished he understood more of the language. Caiaphas was a snake and Herod a rascal.

"He had been surprised when the Jew, Joseph, whom he knew only slightly, had requested audience and then the body of Jesus. Was he already dead? They had waited for the centurion to return and report. 'All three who were crucified today are dead, sir, well dead and no doubt about it.' Pilate had ordered the release of the body.

"During the Sabbath the Jews, including Herod, were about their own business. Pilate was expecting to visit Herod on the first day of the week, a return courtesy call. But before he could leave, even before his breakfast was over, there was that fox, Caiaphas, wanting to see him privately on a matter of *very* urgent business. Most disturbing. He had agreed with the measures Caiaphas was taking. When he had gone, he alerted the duty cohort to stand by. Trouble was likely. He called the centurion who had been on duty at Calvary again and questioned him carefully. What was it the man had said to him before he was taken to the hill outside the city? He tried to remember.

"He told his wife everything. They, in puzzlement, mulled it all through again—and again. Suppose, just suppose, the Man had been telling the Truth.

"Through the week that followed, Pilate's informers reported back. The followers of the Man were rejoicing, *rejoicing!* They had seen him. A*live.* No, it wasn't a ghost. It was Him, A*live.* He had eaten food. He had passed through closed doors. He bore the wounds of the cross. Without being told, he knew things that had happened in his absence. Many had seen him. He covered distances instantaneously. What *was* going on? Pilate was glad the Festival was over and he could return to Caesarea.

"And then there was Thomas. Thomas was the one who was

missing that first evening, remember?

> "Then the same day at evening, being the
> first day of the week, when the doors were shut
> where the disciples were assembled for fear of
> the Jews, came Jesus and stood in the midst, and
> saith unto them, Peace be unto you. And when
> he had so said, he shewed unto them his hands
> and his side. Then were the disciples glad, when
> they saw the Lord. Then said Jesus to them again,
> Peace be unto you: as my Father hath sent me,
> even so send I you. And when he had said this, he
> breathed on them, and saith unto them, Receive
> ye the Holy Ghost:

"Now remember what Jesus does this first day. They are behind locked doors for fear of the Jews. The hunt to locate them is already on. Suddenly, without warning, Jesus stands in the middle of them. They have no time to work out how he does it for he is speaking. 'Shalom.' It is *His* voice all right. He holds out his hands to them, holds them out close. He turns so that they can all see, and so the light of the oil lamp falls clear on the palms of his hands. They flinch as they see how large the holes have torn. The flesh is red and raw. He is clothed. He pulls back the loose tunic robe and again there is indrawn breath of pain as each of them sees the size of the bloodied wound where the spear was thrust. Crowding into their minds, with no time to give them coherence, are thoughts flashing without sequence—'He's *Alive!*' 'He didn't die after all.' 'He's escaped.' 'How did He get here?' 'I saw him die!' 'What does it mean?' Tumbling memories of things He had said so recently crowd upon them, and begin making sense. They look at Peter. He is on his knees. They too, awed and frightened, not understanding, drop to their knees. The nail holes in his feet catch their eyes.

"Jesus is pale and intense, urgent. He is giving them the charge: 'As my Father hath sent me, even so send I you.' He now blows on all of them, turning full circle that none be missed. They feel the moving air on their heads. 'Receive ye the Holy

Ghost. Whose soever sins ye remit, they are remitted unto them; and whosoever sins ye retain, they are retained.' He holds his hands out over them, blesses them and, as suddenly as He came, is gone. Their eyes hold each other in wonder, in surprise. Then, following Peter's look, turn to the door. The wooden bar across the door from jamb to jamb is still in place, undisturbed.

> "But Thomas, one of the twelve, called Didymus, was not with them when Jesus came. The other disciples therefore said unto him, 'We have seen the Lord.' But he said to them, 'Except I shall see in his hands the print of the nails, and put my finger into the print of the nails, and thrust my hand into his side, I will not believe.'

"There is always the implication that Thomas' faith was somewhat less than the other disciples. We use the phrase 'Doubting Thomas' to suggest unworthy, unwarranted doubt. This is surely a slur on a remarkable man. God gave us minds to use, and reason to exercise. Thomas doubted for very good reason. He had not been there when the others had encountered Jesus. They had all, not only seen him, but had seen him in circumstances that did not permit doubt. Had any of them also not been there, they too would have responded as Thomas did.

"Thomas' story is essentially the story of three responses— his own two responses and that of Jesus. His initial response on hearing this fantastic story from his friends was the normal, sane, reasoned response that any man or woman with feet on the ground would make. What was he faced with?

"Jesus had died on the cross. Yes, Thomas knew that. Standing on the wall at a distance, holding his silence and checking back his tears, he had seen him die, die slowly, and had seen him taken down and, eventually, taken away. Yes—the body was no longer where it had been buried. Peter and John had confirmed that.

"An angel had told Mary that Jesus was risen. Mary, Peter, and the others had seen Jesus. But what has been seen?

"What has been seen, according to his friends, is not an

apparition, a ghost. Ghosts have no feet. Jesus' feet had nail holes in them. What they were saying they had seen was the solid, physical, substantive presence moving about, without assistance, of a man who had died; a man out of whose body life had departed. And that beloved man passed through locked doors. Or He appeared from God-alone-knew-where in the midst of his disciples who were behind locked doors. And He had shown them his wounds, the wounds of the cross. He had invited them to touch him and they could have reached out and done so had there been any doubt—but there they had not because there was not. He had been hungry and they had given him the last piece of fish on the platter, and a piece of honeycomb. He had eaten it, all of it, breaking it into morsels with his torn hands while they watched, in awe and in silence.

"It must have been some kind of group hallucination—or was it?

"We are all like Thomas. Confronted by an impossibility, we tell it like it is. We live foreshortened and limited lives by our own choices. Because God has to work within our own chosen parameters for Him, we cannot, do not, see the miraculous around us or recognize the presence of God when it is there. We put down conditions for God to work by or within. Our service, our obedience, our responses are conditional or provisional. We qualify our obedience and qualify its measure. We will do something *if* God will do something. We bargain with God with the presumptions of a child bargaining over the amount of his pocket money with his father.

"I have done it. You have done it—and we continue to do it.

"God, if you will ... heal Dad, then ...

"If you will ... show me yourself, then ...

"If you will ... give me the gift of .... then ...

"If you will ... bring him (her) back, then ...

"Oh, how we love putting out fleeces. And it is often not led of God, but in ignorance, a perplexity, a puzzlement, that would otherwise border on arrogance. An arrogance that persuades us that we and God are partners, even if we are junior partners, in a holy enterprise.

"I have made my bargains with God—if you will do this, God, then I will do that – and I have lived to regret them. But the breathtaking wondrous thing is that the Creator of the Universe, author of the Big Bang that started Creation, and He who alone knows when it will end, has accepted the challenges from this speck of dust that is me, and has responded to me on *my* terms.

"Just as Jesus did to Thomas.

"I find myself asking: was the reason that Jesus returned on the eighth day because He wanted to make sure of Thomas? Was Thomas that important to him that He, the risen Christ, should come back a second time to the same place, at the same time, in similar circumstances, where the only difference was that this time Thomas is present! And his transactions, this time, are solely with Thomas.

"The two narratives, set a week apart, are remarkably similar. Jesus reappears, greets them in the same way, and turns immediately to Thomas.

> "And after eight days again his disciples were within, and Thomas with them: then came Jesus, the doors being shut, and stood in the midst, and said, Peace be unto you.

"Come with me now, shhhhh, quietly slip back past the centuries. Let us stand in the corner opposite the lamp where we won't throw shadows. All movement, all conversation, has stopped. It is like a moment in time frozen onto a photograph. A few disciples sit on low stools. The others, except two who are standing, sit on the floor. Some rest their backs against the wall. Others prop themselves on an elbow. Jesus, indisputably it is He, is in the center among them. He does not appear to see us.

> "Then saith he to Thomas, 'Reach hither thy

finger, and behold my hands; and reach hither thy hand, and thrust it into my side: and be not faithless, but believing.'

"Thomas had laid down the conditions for his belief. Jesus is responding, *on Thomas' terms.*

"We are on the edge of a mystery here of the nature and character of God that we have no time to explore. For this action parallels the pictures Jesus has painted in his parables of God as a father, patient, and long-suffering. He is responding, as He need not, to the demands of his children. He is the father, yielding to the demands, for instance, of a younger son, dealing with him on the boy's terms. And then later, with the older son, pleading for a right response. The fathers, in Jesus' stories, though they certainly have authority, are all subject to the whims and refusals of their children.

"Jesus holds out his hands, offers them to Thomas, invites Thomas to reach out his fingers to touch the holes made by the nails. Thomas, wide-eyed and awestruck, does not move. His eyes return to Jesus' face. Once more, Jesus pulls back the folds of his robe. Again, the broad gash, the open wound, and the torn flesh are visible. 'Reach out your hand Thomas, and feel me. Come now, feel. Be absolutely certain.'

"But Thomas doesn't reach out, doesn't feel. Suddenly he breaks. He is on his knees and his head, his hair, are on Jesus' feet. And he is sobbing as though his heart would break. He too has met Jesus face to face. Now he too knows what the others knew. He is seeing suddenly, with shock, and yet with understanding, the true mystery of the Cross. There, every human suffering and every human evil was focused into the one event in all of history that makes sense of it all. An event that he, Thomas, had recently watched. Now, for the first time, it becomes illuminated by comprehension. The light and warmth of the sun may focus into a point of intense heat and brightness. So too, in the torn hands and side of the risen Christ, he sees all the wrong and injustice of human history, the agonies and grief of the human race, focused on that lone, unique sufferer before him.

"The time perspective of our lives is not the small, limited world of working or middle-class life that we consider to be ours. It is, instead, a cosmic stage on which the great extremes of the Gospel, perceived by more than reason, are stark realities. Reason cannot bring into congruence light and darkness, life and death, satiety and starvation, heaven and perdition.

"In this struggle of immense opposites, those torn hands are raised to their true height. God, in order to save us, has made available, in that stricken side and those pierced limbs, His divine wisdom and strength and love.

"And Thomas answered him and said unto him, My Lord and my God.

"Nowhere in the Gospels is there a stronger affirmation of who Jesus is than we hear Thomas make. Peter at Caesarea Philippi had cried out 'Thou art the Messiah, the Son of the Living God.' But there were many meanings for the word Messiah and they did not necessarily mean divinity.

"Thomas has neither doubts nor qualifiers to utter. He knows for certain—Jesus is Lord!

"When people talked of a Lord, they referred to temporal power. It was a common title of the Roman emperor. Lord meant world ruler, ultimate force, absolute control. But this is not the sense in which Thomas uses it, attributing ultimate power to Jesus. No, he is saying simply and with total honesty and intent 'Jesus, from this moment You are my Lord. From now on the controlling power in my life is You! My Lord and my God!'

"The realization was staggering. The crucified Jesus is the only accurate picture of God the world has ever seen. The almighty power of suffering, self-limiting love is the picture of God's omnipotence that He wishes us to see, and grasp, and hold. We must be willing, as Thomas was, to have our understanding of God modified, even revolutionized, by what we learn of Him in Jesus Christ.

"Tradition says that some time before the year AD 48, a tired and dusty traveler called Thomas, a Jew and a follower of Jesus, made his way to Taxila. Thomas' passion for this man called Jesus led to the establishment of a small Christian community. Sixty years ago a cross dating from the second century was unearthed there and has become the symbol of the present day Church of Pakistan. It is said that Thomas went back down the Indus River by barge to the South Indian Peninsula. There he founded a church still known today by his name—the Mar Thoma Church. It is without a doubt one of the oldest existing church communities for which continuity can be traced. It is believed that Thomas was martyred there.

"I had said there were four people I wanted to talk about. Abide with me just a wee while more.

"We are still in that upper room with the barred door. We have heard Thomas' broken cry, 'My Lord and my God.' But now Jesus stoops to raise Thomas back up to his feet, speaks softly to him, and then … He turns and He sees us! He turns towards us, more specifically toward you, clad so incongruously in your twentieth century clothes, and feeling so much a stranger among the others. He steps forward to stand immediately before you. Yes, you. And in the silence, thick enough to cut with a knife, holds out his hands toward you, turns the palms upwards, looks directly at you…and waits. It is the eighth day after Easter for you, too. And He is waiting …waiting for your response."

Two Commandments

The two commandments are found in Luke 10:27 NIV

Love the Lord your God with all your heart
and with all your soul and with all your strength
and with all your mind;
and, Love your neighbor as yourself.

K en feels the two commandments are in the right sequence. Man must love God in order that he may adequately love his neighbor. His neighbor loses if he does not love God enough. Much of the pain in the church derives from lack of lovingness towards God reflected in lack of personal loveliness.

The church always exists in an alien society. The situation for Christians in Pakistan is not unique. By its very nature, its relationship with the world around it is uneasy. The claims of society take many forms and are inevitably set off against the claims of Christ for those who follow Him. The strain is always there and in the tension some will crumble and others reach the heights where saints are born.

Ken wants the eighties be a decade of discipleship for Christians, a time of proving His promises. It should be a time of learning how to love Him as He demands to be loved, to seek His indwelling and empowering. The witness of Christ should be *in* every Christian. He writes a poem on prayer.

Prayer is a goal, not just a way,
Itself is whole, enough to pray,
Not then to wait, but then to rise.
The day demands *our* enterprise.

The building research and development center attached to CTTC has no budget. Yet somehow finances itself and gives work to about 20 young men. Some make prefabricated parts for buildings that will be used in the housing colony across the road. Others make steel door and window frames and concrete molds.

CTTC itself is involved in many different programs. The Government wants to implement a program immediately for the manufacture of concrete water control gates for irrigation channels. These will make better use of limited water supplies in one of the largest irrigation systems in the world. Ken is developing new manufacturing techniques to meet their needs.

A tall, genial American and a young Filipino half his size are using new wet and dry rice farming techniques to double rice production in what was once the rice bowl of India. For them, Ken's students have been making line markers to guide the planting of rice in rows.

For the international rice research institute, CTTC is hurriedly copying rice planters brought in from the Philippines.

For Dr. Zafar, a beloved young Pakistani doctor, there is need for a prefabricated septic tank for the villages of his rural health project. But first there is a need for drains. In one village the many milk buffaloes daily churn the narrow lanes into quagmires—sometimes thigh deep. One bearded old man said it has been 30 years since he last walked up the lane with shoes on. CTTC completed a survey for a drainage system. Then came estimates and agreement with the villagers to share the task. This spring Paul and Jamie, two English teenagers, went off nervously to Ahmalpur.

Ken visited after heavy rains recently. What a transformation! Every lane was dry. Water gurgled down open single-brick drains towards the ponds outside the village. Women cleaned the drains outside their mud houses. Householders brought donkey loads of sand to cover their courtyards, creating clean, sustainable walking paths. A whole village smiles. Many neighboring villages clamor for drains, 27 at last count. Now for the septic tanks!

Ken is preparing to lay the foundation stone for the dreamed of Building Trades Center. The $10 an English visitor gave him three years ago has grown to $25,000 after a gift by the Canadian Ambassador. This will be the only school in the country of this type and will cost nearly one million dollars. The government authorities watch with interest to see what happens—how the school is paid for.

On May 2nd, there are two birthdays. One is Ken's. He is 55. The important one for him is the founding of Yahovah Shalom. This is the name chosen for the retreat center in Jhelum. It means 'The Lord's Peace'.

The center is presently a skeleton. It is dilapidated and run down. The U.P. Church, USA has agreed to make it available for a spiritual ministry. He needs help for it to become a place of God's peace where men, women, and young people can be refreshed and helped spiritually. The work of repair and re-equipment will proceed as he receives donations from his network of friends and churches. They are asked to help join in this ministry as the Lord leads. Mostly he wants prayer that it will come into being. He also asks for prayer for a young couple—Aslam Ziai, and his wife, Sudaish. They have committed themselves to this ministry, but will need help from others. So Ken also asks for prayer the Lord will send people of His choice. The first retreat will be a pre-Sialkot Convention prayer retreat in mid-September.

Ken and Marie are given furlough every five years. However, it's been 12 years since they took one. The plan for the 1982 furlough is to spend a month in England. Their son, Colin, is studying first year engineering in London and they will get to spend some time with him. Unfortunately, their other son, Tim, his wife, Cathy, and their darling daughter, Anna, are somewhere with 'Youth With A Mission', possibly in Israel. So they will miss getting to see them.

Then in the US, their base will be in Richland, Washington for the remainder of their time. Ken is never comfortable being away from his work, and expects to return to Pakistan for several short spells even though he's supposed to be on furlough.

Thanksgiving

Ken is English and doesn't celebrate Thanksgiving, although he finds much to be thankful for. From healed relationships to God's ample provision in so many ways, he rejoices and gives grateful thanks to God.

Ken rejoices that, after a lapse of four years, a Synod meeting of the United Presbyterian Church is being held in Pakistan. In previous years, there were unresolved divisions cause by stubbornly held views in different areas. After persistent, wise, and loving mediation by the American representative, Woody Busse, almost all delegates attended a peaceful meeting. Gujranwala was the second mission station of the USA church. It once bustled with missionaries, but now Ken and Marie, who are 'adopted' Presbyterians, are probably the last of a long line. Marie, with 35 years in Pakistan behind her, would like to retire, but Ken is still chasing dreams and racing against time. He subtly changes the conversation to more immediate goals.

Ten years ago, funds to rebuild CTTC were secured. Now the last building is going up, inside another. With no scaffolding available, the old office building is being replaced by a two-story building built inside it. The new roof beams will rest on the existing roof until the concrete sets and then, brick by brick, the old building will be peeled away to be used elsewhere.

From his original goal of 250, there are now 400 boys enrolled. He can't thank God enough. From a goal of 100 graduates per year, in just the last four years they have sent out 640 Christian boys across this land who are trained craftsmen. Many have gone to the Middle East oil countries. These young men have been nurtured by Bible classes, morning chapel, camps at Shalom Center, and programs with special speakers. All this has prepared them to effectively witness the vitality of their faith. A boy's stay here, in a loving and nurturing environment, becomes for him a leap from a morass to a strong rock revealing long, bright horizons.

Ken's leadership in CTTC draws to a close. He is confident that a suitable Pakistani replacement can be found.

In recent years, school expenditures have threatened to outstrip income. But each year God has covered all needs. Fees remain at a level that most, although not all, poor Christian rural families can meet. The actual cost of training a peasant's son to be a draftsman, or a sweeper's son to be a welder, or a field laborer's son to be an electrician, is a mere $8.65 per month! Where else can such value in improved quality of life be achieved at so little cost?

Over the years Ken has reduced admittance requirements. Boys without schooling learn to be carpenters as they learn to read and write their own language. He has long had a burden for that great body of youngsters whose intelligence has never been challenged and honed by formal schooling.

In the last five years, the bank account for the Building Trades Center has steadily grown. Although costs for the school have increased dramatically, there is now $587,000 cash in land, and promised support so he is more than 40 percent of the way toward the need of $1,388,000. Isn't God just *so good*?

The foundations of the first building have been poured. The new school, being built on land adjacent to CTTC, will teach 350 boys construction trades. Boys without previous education will become brick layers, plasterers, painters, plumbers, pipe-fitters, concrete laborers, and steel rebar benders.

Another new school is even further along. The double story building under construction will house the English Language

Institute. If the people in rural Christian communities are to progress, it is essential they gain more than usual competence in English. Although Pakistan has been independent for 35 years, the effective language of government and commerce is still English from the time it was part of the British Empire.

Ken is now looking for a Principal who is experienced in teaching English as a foreign language. And he needs volunteers who will come for a year to help. They would teach college students, local school teachers, trainees, seminary students, business men, and educated upper class women. Ken envisions running classes morning, afternoon, and evening, which means it will soon have more students than CTTC. There will probably never be a better opportunity to reach out into the heart of the city. If possible, he wants to start next April.

Ken and Marie have had several young volunteers this year. Nine youngsters from 'Youth With A Mission' brought their joy and enthusiasm into their lives. Three others are presently at Shalom Christian Center in Jhelum where Rennie and Melloney Gold strive to turn the old Mission Hospital into a center for deeper spiritual life. It is a massive task, but God covers the needs as they reach out in faith.

Court cases are a part of life. When they returned from furlough last year, Ken went undercover until he could get bail before being arrested. He is accused of embezzling $3,000 from the Bible Medical Missionary Society. This fictitious case has been brought by nominal Christians he has never met who are trying to extort money from the Society for Community Development. They mistakenly thought he was their property manager. Much time has been consumed in traveling to Lahore, 45 miles away. In multiple hearings in five different courts, he still hasn't heard any evidence.

Once again, Ken looks forward to Advent and Christmas with great expectancy. It is a great adventure that He, the Son, initiated and exemplified.

A Well-Deserved Award

Ken has been nominated to receive an OBE. which stands for Officer of the British Empire. He receives a letter from the British Embassy in Islamabad dated January 5th, 1984.

> Mr. Kenneth G Old OBE
> Principal
> Christian Technical Training Center
> Gujranwala

Dear Mr. Old,

We have spoken on the phone about your OBE, but I have not yet had an opportunity to give you my warmest congratulations in writing. It is certainly a great tribute to all the work you have done in Gujranwala over the years. And we in the Embassy are delighted at the news.

How would you like to receive the OBE? If you are going to be in the UK this year you could go to one of the Investitures at Buckingham Palace. The spring dates are 14, 21 and 28 February and 6, 13 and 20 March. It may be difficult at this short notice to arrange for you to attend in February. If you cannot make the spring dates, there are other Investitures in the summer (usually two dates in July) and autumn (late October, November and early December). We shall be getting the exact dates in due course. If you are interested in attending an Investiture at Buckingham Palace could you fill in the attached form which we will forward to the Foreign and Commonwealth Office. This ought to be done by the end of this month. The address in the UK could be any accommodation address; it is simply the place where they send the formal invitation just before the ceremony.

The alternative is for the Ambassador to deliver the award to you, once the Insignia arrives in about March. He could do this at a short and informal ceremony either in Gujranwala or here in Islamabad at any time that suits you. He will be back next week.

Please let me know what you would prefer.

Yours Sincerely
Anthony Goodenough

He also receives a letter from The Director-General, Sir John Burgh, at the British Council in London.

Mr. Ken Old OBE
The Technical Training Center
c/o The British Council
Lahore, Pakistan

PERSONAL

Dear Mr. Old,

We were delighted to see that you have been made an OBE in the New Year Honours List. On behalf of the British Council I send you our warmest congratulations.

Council staff in Pakistan and from London, who have visited the Technical Training Center, have recognized that your work there has established a unit which is a model of how really practical technical training can be carried out, with a minimum of financial resources. We remember with gratitude the help you gave us in developing the concept of the library in Lahore, which led to our being able to construct an excellent building at remarkably low cost.

We offer our best wishes, to yourself and to all at the Center, for 1984.

Yours Sincerely
John Burgh

Another letter comes from H. L. Hayat at the Urdu Bazar in Sialkot

Dear Mr. K. G. Old,

I have just this morning heard from Dr. K. Lall a good news that you have been awarded by British Government the honour of OBE.

My family, friends, Rani, Prof Tony Hayat, Prof. Julliana Hayat and Janis Hayat join you and Mrs. Kenneth Old in your happiness. It is a great honour to Old family, as well as to all those who know that you and Mrs Old are an asset to us all.

We would as a family would feel honoured if you allow us to hold a function in your honour. Where would you wish it to be held—Sialkot or Gujranwala? I think Gujranwala would be a better place as I wish to invite the Commissioner, The D.M.L.A., D.C. and S.P. of Gujranwala to the function.

You may be having some fear by any adverse report to the Government by some foolish friends. I will always stand by you and any other missionary or Fraternal workers, whether any one of them likes me or not.

I have done this in case of Reed family and Dr. O. L. Hamm. I regret nationals did wrong information into the ears of foreign Church workers to know what is right and what is wrong.

Anyhow, please let me know the place you wish to hold this small function. I would welcome any number of your friends to the get-together.

Best regards to you and Mrs. Old.

Yours Sincerely.
H. L. Hayat

A further letter comes from missionary friends in Islamabad.

Dear Ken and Marie,

Thank you, dear people, for the warm greeting on our arrival here. It is so good to be back since we never stopped traveling, really, during our home assignment. (Shades of the Olds!)

Yes, we have heard some of the horrendous

new developments of the Church in Gujranwala. May the Lord deliver us. Have you ever considered withdrawing and having nothing to do with the messes? Even the Lord sometimes (not lightly) gives up (Romans 1) and what worse condemnation can there be than when God turns away? However, I know that your keen devotion and sense of responsible nature will reject this, but let's debate it– which leads to my next point.

I need to touch base with you in order to get back into the pattern of institution management. What is your schedule? I come to Lahore Jan. 24 – 26 for the MCS Board. Is it possible for me to proceed to Gujranwala on the 27, say, for a confab, stay the night and then return to Rawalpindi on the 28th?

Congratulations, Sir Kenneth, on the OBE. May we offer you beds if you can come here to receive the award? Let us know.

Well done thou good and faithful servant!!! K.P.O.

Bob (and Rowena)

Note: K.P.O. is an expression Ken uses meaning 'Keep Pressing On'.

An insert in the Walnut Creek church bulletin in California is dated 2/19/84

KEN OLD RECEIVES
THE ORDER OF THE
BRITISH EMPIRE

In 1971, Presbyterian Missionary, Ken Old dreamed a dream…the dream of a vocational school for underprivileged boys in Gujranwala, Pakistan. God honored the dream as well as Ken's persistence and dedicated work. He turned it into a Christian Technical Training Center, a model institution, where over 400 boys study. It is a school which succeeds where similar Government-operated schools do not...a sort of 'Boys Town', creating opportunities for dropouts, deprived and delinquent boys. These boys, seizing their opportunities, have little time for riots, burning busses or public property. One of them is now the Principal. The staff is described as being imbued with loyalty, service, dedication, motivation, commitment and innovation. High praise, indeed, in any framework!

This week we received the following from Marie:

Ken was given a great honor when his name was included in the Queen's New Year Honours List. The London Times says he was awarded "The Order of the British Empire for education and community service in Gujranwala, Pakistan." We were very surprised and don't know how it came about except that people from the British Embassy often come here and have been observing the work for years so one of them must have recommended it. Now they ask if Ken would like to go to Buckingham Palace to receive it from the Queen or would he like the Ambassador to come here to give it, or would he like to go to Islamabad to receive it. We think we will ask him to come here so the entire staff can share in the honor as without them the work would be impossible.

We at Walnut Creek add our praise and thanksgiving for this great honor. To God be the Glory! Great things He hath done.

In February another letter comes from the British Embassy in Islamabad.

Dear Mr. Old,

Many thanks for your letter of 12 February. I am glad that I was just able before going on leave to warn you of the award of the OBE and I am delighted that while I was away it all went through without a hitch. Very many congratulations.

I should be very happy to visit you in Gujranwala and give you the award at whatever sort of ceremony you would like. It will give me another opportunity to have a look around the Center. As soon as the Insignia arrives, I will get in touch about a date that suits us both.

Yours Sincerely,
Oliver Forster

In March, the award arrives.

Dear Mr. Old,

I have now received your OBE and am ready to deliver it to you whenever it is convenient. I myself am likely to be tied up with a Ministerial visit and with the Cricket Team until after 23 March. So any time towards the end of this month or in April (or even later if you preferred) would suit me. Let me know in due course what would suit you.

Yours Sincerely,
Oliver Forster

The Award Ceremony

In April the British Ambassador arrives to present Ken with his OBE. Christians and Muslims from all over the village gather to show their support and appreciation for Ken. He's well loved and respected and all are eager to share in the joy of the occasion. Chairman Rehmat Ali Bagri gives the Address of Welcome:

> We are honored at the presence among us of so many distinguished guests—our Mayor and members of the Municipal Committee, members of our District Councils, distinguished citizens of our city, our officials who serve us, our Commissioner, Deputy Commissioner and Superintendent of Police and members of their staffs.

> We are gathered to greet our distinguished guests, the Ambassador of the United Kingdom, Sir Oliver Forster, and to share in the ceremony he has come to Gujranwala to perform.

> We are glad of the occasion for several reasons.

> First, because it has brought the Ambassador not through Gujranwala, but to Gujranwala. Travelers, because of our proximity to Lahore, tend to take either the bypass to the east or the bypass to the west of our city. Alternatively, they fly *over* Gujranwala. Rarely is this city the

destination of the traveler.

And yet we are proud of our city.

We are one of the major cities of the Punjab, one of the fastest growing in population. It will not be long before we exceed one million people. We are an industrial city with several thousand industrial units. We are an agricultural center and a communications hub. We have recently become a Divisional Center under our first Commissioner, Mr. G.M. Piracha, who is here among us.

We are glad, too, for the occasion that has brought the Ambassador to us. He has come to honour one of Gujranwala's citizens of which we are proud. Mr. Old may be a British citizen, but both he and his wife belong to Pakistan and to us.

The year 1947 was the year our country of Pakistan was born and the dreams of millions of our people came true. A nurse in the United States who had served through the war in Africa and Italy was asked if she would go for not more than a year to assist the increasing number of Muslim refugees fleeing westwards across India towards the land of safety, Pakistan. She formed part of a team that met streams of our people near Ferozepur and traveled with them giving medical care and help as they trudged towards Lahore.

I have no doubt there are people in Gujranwala today who have reason to be grateful for the love and concern they received from that medical team in 1947. Three of them lost count of time. 30-seven years later they are still here. Dr. and Mrs. Christy are in Taxila where Dr. Christy has earned a worldwide reputation as an eye surgeon. Mrs. Old is here among us today and we honour her for the service to our people for more than half her lifetime.

In 1947 Mr. Old was a young officer in the Royal Engineers serving in Waziristan. On August 15th he handed over his duties to his Pakistani colleague. Less than a year ago, some 36 years later, he again handed over his duties, this time as Principal of the Christian Technical Training Center, to his Pakistani colleague, Mr. Nathaniel Newab, whom he now assists.

We who live here in Gujranwala had become aware of strange things happening in our midst. An educational institution of high quality was developing. Mr. Old, knowing nothing about educational techniques when he came here in 1970, applied an engineer's mind freshly and freely to the challenge of educating young men. He is an educational radical, seeing the unsuitability of many Western norms of education for a developing country and seeking to find fresh solutions suitable to our needs.

When we were boys, the school was called the Boys Industrial Home. It then became the Christian Technical School. The building up of the new Christian Technical Training Center has been for Mr. Old a consuming task. It has grown to almost 500 boys. More than 200 young craftsmen graduate annually. They come not only from our own city, but from all over the Punjab and beyond. Now there are boys in Africa who would like to study here. Townspeople send their sons there because they receive sound teaching, develop skills and are *disciplined*. Boys need discipline and our nation needs disciplined people.

The Christian Training Technical Center is known as a school for dropouts. It has *no* educational requirements for admission. Some boys learn to read and write their own language of Urdu alongside learning skills as carpenters. The CTTC has few parallels, but it is effective and its graduates find jobs!

There are phrases of English that we Pakistanis use that would appear strange to foreign ears. We talk about 'missionary dedication' and 'missionary zeal'. We have learned to use those adjectives because of people like Mr. and Mrs. Old.

We, too, honor them today and thank them for their service to our city.

The Ambassador presents Ken with a certificate hand-signed by the Queen and a gold medal. From now on, Ken often signs his name, especially on important documents, as Kenneth G. Old OBE.

CTC Expands

Ken is never satisfied with the success of educating people. He not only wants the village children to be educated, but their parents as well. He wants to provide higher education for those who may have been to school, but could benefit from further learning. He wants every person to have an opportunity to better themselves, from the housewife to the business man. Everyone can benefit from one type of schooling or another. He now has a fifth school operating.

Ken and Marie go on furlough at the end of 1984. They spend

time with Colin in England. He has completed his two-year assignment in London as drafting instructor. When they go to the States, he goes with them. He has applied for an immigrant's visa and wants to make a life for himself in the States.

They spend Christmas with Tim and Cathy at their 'Youth With A Mission' home base in Virginia. Granma Marie spoils them rotten. Ken leaves a few scattered fairies in hiding places that only Anna and Debbie know. Tim and his family will be going with their discipleship training students to the southern Caribbean for evangelistic outreach. He will take another group to London in the summer. Cathy expects their third child next March so the spring outreach to Chile next year will be without them.

On their return in February, Ken is soon immersed in the Gujranwala Education Center. He will soon have to retire. With both boys in the States, it will be hard for them to think of retirement anywhere else. They do have a home in England, however. For Ken, it's difficult to think of retirement at all. He is in pursuit of more dreams than ever, and fights against the march of time.

Marie dreams other dreams—of rest and relaxation, of summers warm, not beastly hot, and not being mother to a whole community.

However, they do share a dream. It's that God purposes to see created in this city of theirs, although maybe not in their time here, an educational ladder for the people that may one day become a university.

The nucleus is the Christian Technical Training Center. Ken is now making alterations so that girls can be admitted. Also, that the new course in electronics can be opened. Alongside this are three new institutions—The Building Trades Center, The English Language Institute, and the Barr Training Institute.

The Barr Training Institute is named after James Barr, the first missionary to Gujranwala. This institute follows no set educational pattern, but offers part-time courses in computers, cooking, watercolor painting, French, shorthand, electricity, accounting, bookkeeping, and running a small business. The aim is to create interest in what is available to the people for further education.

The Building Trades Center, longer in the dreaming, is now a reality in the first of its own buildings. Ken took 70 of the neediest boys at CTT —the carpenters— and is busy organizing them into a school that will one-day rival CTTC itself. Because many of them have little previous schooling, they only have two classroom lessons a day apart from Bible. After that it's practical work. Boys, grouped in pairs of a senior and a junior, are off to work—lopping trees, shifting timber, sawing logs, building forms for concrete. And they help pour the concrete. They polish, finish, repair, and make tables, desks, chairs, doors, windows, and coffins. He hopes they will also be making toys and, taught by a Kashmiri woodcarver, be hand-carving furniture and wooden gifts. Eventually this will lead on to another dream—helping the poor run their own business through a bank of their own.

Ken is ahead of the world in providing micro-business opportunities. It will be many years before this 'new' idea makes its way to the African continent. Another innovation he institutes is small business banking. There is no end to the ideas he has for developing the potential of every Christian in the city and nearby villages.

The poor are frequently trapped in their poverty with no way out because no one will lend them money or assistance to escape from it. Ken has done the arithmetic and feels they should now be able to lend money to finance income earning enterprises of the poor, particularly those of our own community. Our three British accountants, a superb team and an answer to prayer, are stretched already, but are willing to try running a bank also. The bank will provide initiatives, management advice, and credit funding for small entrepreneurs. He would like products suitable to manufacture for local or overseas markets.

In addition to the individual business opportunities, he creates greater dimensions by instituting the small industries project. He intends to help the people establish small production and service industries. He will give them the counsel, backing, and encouragement necessary for them to be successful. Part of the CTTC metal trades shop will be used to manufacture and sell whole prefabricated buildings of steel. The trainees, working under student management, will share in the profits.

Recently, his time has once again been taken up with the embezzlement case, now in its fifth year. Last summer his lawyer, now his ex-lawyer, failed to attend the court hearing. In his absence, an adverse judgment based on a forged signature was given holding Ken liable. He is now trying to appeal this. But he continues to thank God for so many assurances of His loving hand.

Ken is always grateful for the gifts from friends and sponsors who bless them with prayer, giving, and labor. The gifts come just in the nick of time to wonderfully fuel what goes on in Gujranwala. And there are the volunteers who come to help. Carl from the U.S. worked for six months as Chief Instructor. Then there was George, 60 years old from England, leaving a secure job to follow Colin as head of the drafting department. Good friends, Piet Born from Holland have promised help. And Phil Gray from the UK will take over, God willing, two of Ken's jobs next year. A young computer major from Washington State is coming to help in the computer school. He is encouraged by the growth in his Pakistani colleagues coming to replace him.

This 'Boys Town' moves on constantly into other areas of service consistently focused on the goal that 'we shall assist the Christian community, in its life and work, to witness to the saving grace of Jesus Christ.'

Village Churches
and Schools

K en and a colleague have been visiting Christian communities across the Punjab, about 120 so far and the same to go. In February, 1986 the Presbyterian Church USA, develops a program for assisting village congregations to repair, complete, or build their churches. This is being financed by the sales of unused Mission property.

It has been quite an education. Sadly, these villages suffer the consequences of political division and enmity within the church leadership. As a result, there has been a widespread movement into the Catholic Church, whose pastoral ministry is orderly and effective. It's a church that offers much to a people in a minority who are discouraged impoverished, needing leadership, and security.

An average church is about 20 feet long and 13 feet wide, with an earth floor and a flat roof that leaks. It has wooden window shutters, and mud walls or bricks laid in mud mortar. Even the task of caring for the churches is overtaxing the resources of some communities. And communities are being diminished as people migrate to the cities in search of work.

Yet the exciting thing is the doggedness and the vitality of those who remain. They are not giving up. They are holding on. In a village of maybe 500 families, perhaps 20 of them go on building their little churches. They fight to keep the rain out and the water buffaloes away from the premises. They struggle against poverty, illiteracy, and rapacious landlords grabbing their cemeteries for more cultivation.

Years ago, a battle with Indian forces swirled around villages near Sialkot. Corpses of soldiers lay still on the ground and vultures wheeled lower and lower in the September sky. In the midst of the uneasy ceasefire, which at any moment might once again erupt into conflict, Ken saw a peasant crossing the field. Walking slowly behind his oxen, he was plowing. Not harvesting, plowing. And it spoke to Ken, and still speaks, of the indomitable courage and patience of the impoverished and oppressed and of a deep unexpressed hope and faith in tomorrow.

Ken asks the villagers, "Do you have any carpet weaving looms?" This means work for the ten-year-old's, but few Christians own a loom. He also wants to know, "Do your children go to school?" Even when government primary schools are available, few children go. They are discriminated against by other children and sometimes even by the teachers too. There is also a sense of "What's the use?"

And so the next question, "Why don't you start your own school?" The parents shrug their shoulders in hopelessness. Ken knows the answer. He was once treasurer for a primary school. The highest fee parents can afford to pay is 30 cents a month. By the time you have taken in enough to pay the salary of a teacher, you have so many children you need two teachers. Then Ken asks, "Suppose you were to receive 400 rupees ($20) each month. Could you run your own school then?"

The situation changes. Hope emerges out of hopelessness. The elders begin talking excitedly. The women join in. A possible teacher's name is suggested. Suddenly things appear to be possible. It's all so humbling. 20 children in a class and it only cost one dollar a month to give each one an education.

Last Friday some of the teachers from the first primary schools came in to receive teaching materials. There are already 200 Christian children enrolled in these schools. Ken supplies them with Bibles and promises a full set of textbooks and teaching charts. For the first time these kids are going to get daily Bible teaching. Ken promises the teachers a month of training each summer to help them improve their skills. He also promises surprise inspection visits. When the children finish primary school, they will be given examinations and scholarships provided for the brightest to attend boarding schools. There are boarding schools for girls but none for Christian boys unless Ken builds one.

His goal is at least 100 schools. There is a question about how they are going to be financed. Ken doesn't know. He only knows that God has laid it on his heart that this is His will for these children and He will surely move the hearts of those who are able to make it possible. He already has sponsors for six schools.

His ultimate dream is to see the young people eventually being able to attend university. There have been recent discussions with the Mission to consider the future development of a Christian University in Gujranwala. Now he's starting a Christian Technical High School using available space in the hostels and in CTTC. The school will be limited to Christian children and will be co-educational. He's busy trying to find syllabuses for what should be taught. None seem to be available even for the government educational system of about ten thousand schools.

The Roofing Factory

The usual exuberance and joy of Christmas is tempered in 1988. There is much concern for the small Christian communities, along with many others, affected by late September floods that devastated many villages not far away.

There is concern too for the government. Pakistan has been in the world news with political changes hardly conceivable at its beginning. It is hoped that the new Prime Minister can steer Pakistan wisely into the future and avoid the errors that end in political disaster. The Punjab province has more than half of Pakistan's 107 million people. Its Chief Minister leads the opposition to Benazir Bhutto. Problems are to be expected and time will tell.

Ken's own life continues to be hectic. A couple of years ago Ken developed a design for a portable building structure to use for Afghan refugees. The roofing itself is a corrugated steel sheet with, if affordable, polystyrene insulation underneath. Its primary use has been on small village churches scattered near and far. The small industries project, started three years ago, is now fabricating, welding, and erecting these steel roofs and buildings. A whole little factory with a pileup of construction orders is the result. Just now Ken is trying to squeeze the manufacture of four church roofs in between three large roofs needed on the campus. This factory has to move out of the Christian Technical Training Center by next March and a new facility must be built.

It was intended to have the new chapel completed by Christmas, but the hostel had to come first. Now the goal is to have it ready for Easter. The local community uses the existing chapel each Sunday. Ken has been moved by their readiness to share in the costs of construction of the new one. The total cost of $29,000 is huge, but about $16,000 is already in hand or assured.

Ken feels so privileged to see the hand of God sharing His goodness over the entire CTTC campus. Almost all the buildings that were here 18 years ago when he first came, have been replaced and enlarged and many new facilities created. There has been a tenfold increase in the number of fulltime Christian students on campus and the rural primary school system has another thousand children.

Ken rarely seems to have any money for his projects. But he is never in debt, and God supplies every need. His dreams continue to increase, but never prove impossible. Although there are still many hurdles to overcome, the first completely Christian College in Pakistan is in the process of becoming a reality. Sadly, Ken will not be around to see its completion as he will be required to retire in two years.

It has been thrilling for Ken to see the responses to the Scholarship program. This is a perpetual scholarship support program for Punjabi Christian children, primarily from rural villages, to enable them to go to boarding school. It's an investment in hope and encouragement and training for Pakistan's future leadership. Each scholarship is invested to produce enough in annual income for both funding a child and increasing the capital. There is need for 700 scholarships.

Ken is rejoicing that in just a year and a half, there are already 116 scholarships! Application forms for attending boarding school in April are now circulating to pastors, teachers, and elders for the next batch of children to be interviewed.

As usual, the praises outweigh the concerns for Ken. Realizing he has been so abundantly blessed by God, he sends a Christmas greeting of blessing to others.

May the sense of God's presence
and His love for us in Christ Jesus
be close to you during this Christmas season
and throughout this New Year.
May He bless you according to your need.

The People of the Punjab

The people in the villages of the Punjab are as varied and unique as those you will find anywhere. From the dedicated teacher in a one room school far from a road to the shoemaker eking out a living repairing the sandals of poor rural families. There is the heartbreak of a farmer who pays very high rent for some land, and sees floods sweep across it during times of very heavy rains. And there is the heartwarming picture of a child sitting on the ground memorizing arithmetic or Bible verses. The pastor of a small church goes around during harvest time collecting the tithes of wheat from his congregation. They are a people who, in the time of oppression, show forth the Love of Christ in their hearts with endurance and strong faith.

Ken and Marie have been members of the Presbyterian Church of Pakistan for more than 30 years. Like any church anywhere there is good and bad, hope and despair, motives and actions high and low. They love their church, hurt for its pain, are supported and encouraged by its strengths, and ministered to by its members. Their church and its people—like life itself—mixes the good and the bad.

Ken's work takes him into villages across the Punjab, a province of about 57 million people. He is involved in more than 400 communities needing help. One aspect of Ken's work is assessing the needs of the churches. When the needs are approved, he is then involved in providing new roofs, even entire buildings. Some congregations are waiting for the 'Mission' to build them a church. Others, with much sacrifice, have already built up to eaves level, and only need a roof. The other aspect of his work is going to check on village schools. In both cases he lives in the closest village until the job is finished.

In the spring of 1989, Ken goes southeast close to the border of India. It is night when he and Evert Lall arrive at the first village. The pastor's small house is full so they stay next door. Their host, Sadar, invites them to go out evangelizing with him in the morning. When they realize this meant 3:30 a.m., Ken feels he has had a long day and declines. Evert does likewise.

Sadar goes alone in the morning. As is his custom, he sings the 23rd Psalm. In his own way, he is taking the Great Commission, "*Go ye into all the world*", into his own smaller world—the narrow, crowded and congested alleyways of his village. For years he has been singing Psalms and hymns in this early morning promenade. At 4:00 a.m. he joins 15 or 20 others for worship and prayers in the church. During his turn on night shift at the railway workshops several miles away, he takes his break from three to five so that his routine is not interrupted.

On one occasion Ken is visiting a village near Pasrur. He discovers that a church elder, using his earnings as a laborer in the steel mill, has managed to buy ten acres of land. The congregation goes to work building a church. Something important, something lively and promising, is happening to these people that have spent so many years in poverty and subjection. They have hope and purpose. They are beginning to acquire means. Now this church too, will soon need a roof.

In another village, however, there is trouble in the Christian community. While attending a wedding, Ken chats with an articulate elder from a small market town. He is looking, in vain, for a middle way. The governing body of the church has split into two factions. In one, a very powerful man has just been elected as moderator for five years, securing his power. In the other, the moderator who recently died has been replaced by his son. The elder is bitter about both. He affirms that almost all the pastors and elders are looking for a middle way separate from both polarized factions. "Please," he pleads, "Don't make any money available to subsidize the income for pastors. That will just lead to votes being bought. Almost all of us are where we are because there is no alternative but to join one of the two parties. Between them they are destroying our church."

Elsewhere, there is trouble of a different kind. Ken goes to a village where there are several churches, and one of them will soon need its roof. Ken sits on a string bed in the home of one of the elders. Elder David explains, "There is divided leadership in our church. Some want to join a church denomination, heavily funded from abroad, that is offering Christian communities a long needed roof in return for their allegiance. All of the smaller groups would rather stay with the American Mission. It is their hospital in Sialkot that cares for us when we are sick. And it is the Mission in Gujranwala that educates our children. It is they who provided roofs to the neighboring villages. And they are the ones our grandparents knew and trusted." Although the American Mission gave way to the United Presbyterian Church of Pakistan more than 30 years ago, memories and loyalties are strong. He makes another plea. "Please, tell your Presbyterian friends in America to become involved again where we are hurting. We need the kind of help they used to give 30 or 40 years ago. We need more missionaries who really know us, listen to us, love us, understand us, and want to work with us. We need people who will stay with us a long time, learn our language, and culture. People who will rebuke us and guide us."

Two churches in a suburb of Gujranwala also need help. One congregation needs to raise and repair the roof and rebuild some walls. The other group has bitten off more than it could chew. The building intended to be used as a school for 100 children is 60 feet by 25 feet. It has walls, but no roof, and they need help. Ken tells them, "Only one can be helped. You must agree between yourselves which one." The little church is now almost finished with a totally reconstructed building.

They also need help for a pastor's house. Ken supplies building materials and roofing, but the pastor's house never seems to get finished. The two rooms are currently being used for straw and water buffaloes. Eventually, the pastor's house is complete, with a courtyard wall for privacy.

The 26 village schools are a joy to Ken. He anticipates adding more. There are more than 900 Christian children enrolled. The 200 Muslim children are only admitted after both parents have been told that Bible is an important part of the program. Small Christian committees, on the edge of their villages, seek help from the Society for Community Development. Help is given, with conditions attached. The local school committee must have two women as well as two men. Women normally only have a background role. The teacher must have ten years of education. There must be at least 25 Christian children on the role and 20 present when the inspection team drops in unannounced. The teachers must go to Gujranwala monthly for their $20 salary. In the summer they attend school themselves for one month. The regular government syllabus is taught.

Ken offers a challenge, not quite sure how he would meet his part of the bargain. The congregation must find $1,000 (WOW!) for roof insulation and somehow Ken will try to find $2,000. That will allow not only for the roof, but for a long verandah along one wall.

Ken and Marie, and the missionaries they worked with the past 30 years, are the last of their kind. They and their friends were committed to serving for the long term. They took time to learn the language and the culture. They were out in the districts from October 'til April. The missionaries really knew the people. They listened and loved unconditionally. They understood the customs and worked among and with the Pakistani Christians. They were not afraid to rebuke when necessary, and made themselves available to give guidance when needed. That was how churches were formed and most of Pakistan's two million Christians can trace roots back to those days.

Now the missionaries are leaving the field, and Ken fears the day of the district missionary is gone forever. The church is becoming a church on the defensive, lacking good leadership, and members no longer attending. Many churches are closing. However, there are the few faithful ones who hold on – like the old man who gathers up a brood of children before dawn to teach them Bible stories. And the elder, who's best hope for someone to succeed him is a former opium addict. All across the Punjab there are hosts of others who stay true, struggling, yet never giving up. And this is the real church.

The Presbyterian Church in Gujranwala, in cooperation with the Presbyterian Church of the U.S., achieves a major landmark. They purchase an expensive church site about 20 square yards for $5,000 on the other side of Gujranwala. It's in a very crowded area where many Christians now live and is the first urban church site bought for many years. There is a rapid influx of villagers to the cities. It is important to acquire building sites before it's too late. The funds for this come from the sale of old Mission land no longer in use.

Ken is encouraged by this help from the Presbyterian Church in the U.S. There are more than 400 requests for help with church buildings or pastors' houses. Now with this new church funding, perhaps the day of the missionary is not over yet.

Although it has been a year of both good and bad, Ken can see, like sunbeams through clouds in a dark sky, the light of God on Pakistan and on the church that He planted there. Ken asks his friends and supporters, "Please pray for the church, its leadership and pastors, and for all the children, thousands of them, with little teaching or learning. And pray that God may be glorified in our own hearts that we all may delight Him with His light in our lives. Pray that God will lead us in the way that we should go."

A Letter from Will

Will Ericson, a former TEAM Missionary and colleague of Ken's while in Gujranwala, writes to sympathize with Ken over his impending retirement. Will has been through it and knows how difficult it is to leave when there are still tasks to be performed. He also recalls the strong character traits he had witnessed in Ken. He had seen the way Ken would stick to his principles and never waver from them. He had watched for any inconsistency in Ken's life, but found none. Ken had preached a sermon, 'Standing on Tiptoe' and that is what Will refers to in his letter.

May 1, 1989

Dear Ken,

I think of you very often and wish I could spend some time with you just to chat and share many of the things that dominate our lives. The few occasions when we could talk alone were very short because of our busyness.

In our memories we seem to think that this is your last year on the field. But even if it will be next year, there must be a number of things going through your mind, both in preparation for leaving and in reflections on what has gone on. It's a tough time that few can share with you.

But, I'm reminded of the modern version of Romans 8:19 that you cited one evening that struck me so forcefully: 'The whole world is standing on tiptoe to see the wonderful sight of the sons of God coming into their own.' You may not have agreed with my view in a contemporary setting, but I do know that many, many have stood on their toes to consider whether you were one of those 'sons of God'. And they have said over and over that you indeed were 'one of those'. I know it for fact because I am one that was encouraged by your steadfastness and integrity.

There are many physical structures that will witness to your work, but, in time, although they have been substantial, they will go the way of most. However, what will endure is the kind of person you were and by what you told so many people in all the so-called mundane things that you did, day-by-day. That is the living legend that will endure far beyond the structures.

You drew a line between, among other things, good and evil. And, I always knew where you were; I could stake my thinking and my activities on it.

And that's why we stood on our tiptoes, to see how you stood up against all the challenges to your integrity. I never saw you cross your line. You may have, but I was never aware of it. Besides, there was only one who ever held the line under all circumstances, and that was Jesus Himself. If some harp at occasional weaknesses, their vision of what life is all about is very narrow.

It's tough to retire. I know. The last few weeks were gruesome. I realized that I could no longer control my long-term efforts. In effect, my power was gone, my plans were no longer viable; first with the long-term, then with the short-term. All of a sudden the time came when what I thought should be done tomorrow didn't count. Almost nothing seemed to count anymore. My replacement didn't need to listen to my advice.

That's when I needed refuge, and even though my ego was severely damaged, I knew that God saw the problem because Jesus had exactly the same experience when His day of 'retirement' approached. I think we can know a little of what was going on in His mind when the day arrived to leave the care and propagation of the Good News in the hands of a few seemingly ignorant and incompetent men.

His solution was to send the Holy Spirit to lead the work.

Your legacy will be to leave your spirit right there, and in league with the Holy Spirit, the important messages will endure—changed lives, questioning minds among the Moslems, the witness to those who stood on tiptoes as you went by. That's really encouraging, isn't it? Nothing's been wasted; no real time has been lost.

Thanks for being a friend. And thanks for accepting the above. In a monologue, you can't argue with me. So, you have to take it as I give it—in a real spirit of love.

All the very best to you and Marie.

Will

Ken's Amazing
Accomplishments

Ken feels God has a great vision for the people of the Punjab. It goes well beyond what he has been able to accomplish in his 20 years at Gujranwala. And what this civil engineer has accomplished is astonishing. Ken has reached retirement age and won't be allowed to continue working. But he has many yet unfulfilled dreams.

Twenty years ago Ken and Marie were working in Taxila Mission Hospital. There he was building an enlarged operation block. Year by year the workload and the opportunity increased. In its now famous operating room, more than 200,000 eye operations have been performed. They both helped in the operating room and loved every minute of it.

But one day they were asked if they would be willing to go and work in a boys' vocational school in Gujranwala, 150 miles to the southeast. Neither of them wanted to leave Taxila and there were many problems in Gujranwala. They hedged their refusal. "We don't know anything about education." But they knew if the Lord wanted them there, He would put them there.

They thought the matter was settled, but six months later, the operating block is not fully complete. Their luggage is on a truck that had recently carried water buffaloes. They are on their way to Gujranwala. Marie is in tears and Ken is thinking, 'I hope the Lord knows what He is doing.'

At that time, there were 60 boys studying drafting, carpentry, radio, auto mechanics and blacksmithing. There is little money available and the options are to close the school, give it to the Government, or try to find out what the Lord wants them to do with this place and its problems.

Ken and Marie had worked in an orphanage in Karachi some 14 years previously. There, to his amazement, he had learned that God is utterly reliable, even from meal table to meal table. And that it was possible to live under the shelter of His constant providing. So, like beggars without bread, he dared to dream of a school rebuilt and reequipped for poor Christian boys, four times as many as the current enrollment. He dreams of graduating 100 boys a year. And he dreams the impossible dream of building hostels where village boys could live while learning a trade and be nurtured in their faith. Ken feels like a penniless spiritual adventurer. When he adds up the figures, he lays before God a shopping list costing $850,000! Within three months he is given the entire $850,000. Now he has to translate vision into reality.

The Society for Community Development is formed. This now manages the work in Gujranwala and is involved in a children's home in Pasrur, a retreat center in Jehlum, an agricultural project in the desert, and a network of village primary schools.

Ken has the feeling he is once again back in 1970 with a vast opportunity reaching out before him, daring him into the future, daring him to trust, and obey.

Ken isn't finished dreaming. He has a vision for the future.

In 1972 the Pakistan Government nationalized privately owned schools and colleges. In one of the miracles of this place, orders that it be nationalized are rescinded after a day of prayer and fasting. That freedom enables him to continue to select the duds and the dropouts, the failures and the kids that just never had a chance. Thousands of underprivileged boys receive training. Christian boys, part of a two percent minority, are encouraged and equipped for life. But nationalization leaves the larger Christian community discriminated against. He mourns the loss of the Christian Training Institute in Sialkot that has trained church leadership for 90 years before nationalization. It is time to do something. The rural primary schools, not limited to Christian children, contribute to this new vision.

About four years earlier, he launched two new institutions. The difference is that they are designed for Christians *only*. The first is a new primary school launched by the local congregation. Almost 300 noisy boys and girls in white uniforms with blue sweaters are using eleven classrooms in the Building Trades Center. Then, two years ago, he started the Christian High School that he envisions will grow into a college. The tenth class is now being admitted and there are 300 Christian students here. These children in both schools get solid Christian teaching every day. Both are co-educational. He recognizes the immense importance these schools will have in the future. There could be more than 500 children in the High School alone, two-thirds of them living in dormitories. The vision just keeps on growing and expanding.

The rural primary schools are going strong. Some 200 miles away, 1,600 children are attending these schools. But then Ken wonders, 'What happens to these kids when they leave primary school?' For this reason, he initiates a new scholarship program. His vision is to have 700 scholarships to provide a chance for schooling to some kid way out there in the distant future. He already has more than 200. Although more children are coming in each day, so far they haven't had to turn any away.

Ken completed the upper floor of Lotze Hostel a year ago. It now has nearly a 100 beds, neatly arranged in four rows. He has promised that in two weeks he will turn over the upper floor of the Brend Hostel which can house another 60 boys. By that time the work on a similar extension to Crowe Hostel will be underway.

This is just a part of the picture. There is still more of his dream.

At the end of this year the first 10th class will graduate. Many of the children will not leave here. Some will move over to the Christian Technical Training Center to take a two-year vocational skills course. They can choose to be a machinist, draftsman, radio & television technician, or hospital technician. Others will continue into eleventh and twelfth grade arts or science studies.

By 1993 those students will be moving into the final two years of their undergraduate degree program, graduating in 1995. One further year could then give them a Bachelor of Education degree also. The degree program could be with either the University of the Punjab or the Open University. There are also possible options for affiliations with accredited overseas educational agencies. A charter as a Minorities College or University is not beyond possibility. A corollary to this degree program, another facet of the vision, would be a nine-month course for primary school teachers following graduation from High School. This would give a well-paid rural job opportunity.

Already this place is unique in its service to the Christian community. Ken feels that what he is already doing is perhaps merely preparing the ground for the future God purposes for this place. That is, *if* they can keep pace with the need for space and scholarships, and the development of programs that this conservative look at the future suggests.

Ken wants to share this vision with others, and asks that they pray along with him that he might not fall short of what God purposes to do for this country and its people. He continues to seek God's will, and finds the unity of the Spirit.

Retirement? – Never!

K en has mixed feelings about retirement. He certainly doesn't intend to retire to an easy chair and do nothing for the rest of his days. He's uneasy about leaving the visions he has for a computer school and his hopes for providing further higher education in the form of a college undone. The number of children in elementary school continues to increase and more classrooms are needed. A hostel needs to be built for the girls. And his dream to build a Modern Town similar to Brend Colony for poor Christian families will never see the light of day.

A memorandum from the Global Mission department of the Presbyterian Church USA confirms that "Kenneth G. Old, after 33 years of devoted service in Pakistan, be honorably retired effective May 31, 1990 and that Marie Old, after 43 years of devoted service in Pakistan, be honorably retired effective May 31, 1990."

Not everyone is happy to see Ken retire. A letter is sent to the Respectable Rev. Ernest Campbell:

> Dear Rev. Campbell,
>
> Christian and cordial greetings. I hope my letter will find you in good condition.
>
> I am Nazir Sardar. I am working at CTTC since 1975, first as an instructor. Then in 1977 I was appointed as a Training Controller in charge of examinations, to maintain the records of the students' homework and class assignments for the various institutes of the SCD. You and your brother visited my office a few weeks ago.
>
> I am not going to tell you about myself, but about another personality.
>
> This was my brief introduction.
>
> The personality which I mentioned above is the Honourable Mr. K.G. Old. He has been serving at SCD campus since 1970 in a very tremendous and titanic way. His work and personality is not limited to work for SCD only, but for many other people and other projects like helping in preparing and erecting church roofs.
>
> Now, according to his age, he is going to be retired in the spring of 1990.
>
> Now I want you to consider my following suggestion and supplication very intently.
>
> 1) People are retired when they are old so they need rest and relaxation according to their

health condition.

A) But I would dare to say that Mr. Old's name is Old, but his work, thinking, gait, physique, assiduity, interest in work, concern for the Christian community is still young in every respect.

B) He is a man of many talents and initiatives which I cannot enumerate them graphically.

C) Honestly, he deserved OBE. which the British Government gave him a few years back.

D) He still works about 10 hours or more daily.

E) He also does the labour work regarding buildings.

F) He has fallen from the buildings a few times, was injured, soon got up and had bandage (maybe he himself or his wife did it, I don't know). Right after that he started the same work. This all for our community.

G) He has a very valuable and creative mind and gives his consultancy to the various other Christian institutions and even to personal cases very happily and readily.

H) Undoubtedly we the staff here say that God has given him some part of the wisdom of Solomon.

I) He established the projects here in such a way that many people got employment and training and education. It is a great help for the advancement and betterment of the Christian community. These projects are a great blessing of God to our Christian people.

J) He has still some projects to accomplish. Therefore, I would request you that please can you do something that he can work here about 2 to 3 years more because he was planning to start a college here for Christians in 1991. There is no college in Gujranwala for Christians. Probably it will be a co-educational college where the girls also come and get benefit of it very easily.

The high school also needs science lab to be established and needs more class rooms as well.

In short, I long to state you that I request that we need him about 2-3 years after his retirement.

If it is a matter of age retirement, then I will say there is a staff member in CTTC who is now 80 years old and still working at CTTC. Mr. Old is 15 years younger than him and much smarter and alert than him so he may be allowed the extension in his services for a few more years which will be great assistance to our Christian community.

Please tell us if you feel our senior staff / principals may request to UPC, USA in the States direct or through you.

I am sending my address as well. I anticipate that you would reply to me in spite of the fact you are very busy in your work.

May God bless you and your family richly.

Yours in Christ,
Nazir Sardar 24/5/89

Despite Nazir's fervent plea, the Presbyterian Church USA ensures that Ken will not be tempted to conclude unfinished business. In a letter dated March 15, 1990 Ken is both complimented and admonished:

Dear Ken and Marie,

Thanks so much, Ken, for coming to NYC for the meeting with your supporting agencies. We all appreciated your sharing with us the present status of the SCD together with your vision for a future project. The work you have initiated is important to all of us. We will do our best to see that it is continued in one way or another, depending, of course, upon the resources available.

As I said to you in the meeting, the Global Mission Ministry Unit is greatly appreciative of the long service that you both have rendered to the mission of our Lord through the Presbyterian Church. Very few missionaries anywhere have demonstrated the selflessness, the compassion, the vision, and the competence that has always characterized your ministry in Pakistan. As with all particular human endeavors, we in the GMMU recognize, however, that changes in personnel must take place. Therefore, we confirm your retirement and departure from the field around the middle of April, 1990. Further, we interpret your retirement to mean that you will no longer have any formal ties with the SCD. For the SCD to request your service in any capacity is an infringement upon your retirement and continues dependency upon your abilities which in the long run is detrimental to the very work you have initiated. Upon retirement, it is appropriate for you to step aside and let others carry on. We encourage you to do just that so that adjustments to your absence can be made as quickly as possible by those who will have responsibility for what takes place in the future.

Because of your retirement, we request that you not make any arrangements to return to Pakistan to undertake any work either with the SCD or with the church roof projects. etc. The roof project will not be closed down, except temporarily until a new builder can be found.

Please do not undertake any additional work unless you can complete the work before you leave. At present, we are hoping that Bill Stump, an engineer who will arrive in mid-July, will find responsibility for the village church project to his liking, and we hope that he will provide leadership for the project.

All of the above does not mean that your insights, experience, and wisdom will be ignored. Rather, it means that you are to be freed of all responsibility to the SCD so that you both can fully enjoy your retirement. The GMMU may, however, ask you to undertake some short assignment to which you are free to respond as you see fit. Further, we do not expect that your interest or your loyalty to the SCD will suddenly cease upon retirement. We hope, however, that your interest and loyalty will be of an informal nature and will support any changes that new leadership might undertake. Again, my personal thanks to you, Ken, for the help you gave to me by coming to New York City. All of us here extend to both of you our gratitude for the many years of service that you have given in the mission of our Lord.

Cordially, Byron L. Haines

Remembering

For Ken's retirement, letters are solicited from the missionaries who worked with him over the years. Apparently, every missionary Ken ever met responded, eager to share some of their own special memories. Although Ken was deadly serious about his work, he had a keen sense of humor. He wasn't what one would think of as a 'typical' missionary. He could charm the children with stories about Little People only half-a-thumb high. He got down on their level, almost becoming a child himself, and included them in the stories. On the other hand, he could offer wise counsel to their parents. Ken is British and quite particular about the way tea should be made and served. But his views were not necessarily shared by Americans. Missionaries are one big family and there is a special bond between them. These letters, selected from the many received, reveal many different facets of Ken's character.

Evelyn Remembers

October 9, 1989

It was 33 years ago this week that we arrived in Karachi after 37 days on a freighter. We were met by Bob Tebbe and taken to the home of Ken and Marie Old where we spent our first night in Pakistan! What a haven that was for two young, scared new missionaries. And what a haven their home has been for us many times since then. I'm not sure that we would have lasted through our first term if it had not been for many, many kind acts from the Olds. There is always a cup of tea, beautifully and lovingly served, and always room for one more at their table.

One summer we lived beside the Olds in Murree. I remember my amazement and respect for this woman who had her house completely settled and a bouquet of flowers on the table within hours of arriving from the plains. She is truly a gracious homemaker.

Of course 'Uncle' Ken is famous for his storytelling. Just recently our son Tim, now himself a father, recalled how he used to look forward to Uncle Ken's stories. "But", he remarked, "I don't think he ever finished one." Tim recalled that Ken had given him seven imaginary monkeys just before we started home on furlough. This kept Tim occupied all during the long trip. He kept the monkeys in the ashtray of the plane seat, and took them out periodically to play with them.

Marie was a very kind and gentle language supervisor when the two of us and the Carlsons were studying Urdu in Sialkot in 1963.

And of course we have all been enriched by the running

debate that was carried on several years ago via the News Notes. Bob Tebbe and Ken were discussing the correct way to make tea. Ken insisted on a brown earthenware pot and putting milk before tea in the cup. Bob, with his PHD in chemistry insisted that these were old wives' tales and could not be proven scientifically.

And then there are the stories about Ken's housekeeping (or lack of it) while Marie was away in Murree during the summer. The legend is that he would not allow a servant in the house. I remember particularly his tale about trying to find an efficient way to wash fruit. It seems that he put a lot of peaches into the washing machine along with detergent and water—one of his less brilliant ideas I believe.

Although Ken and Marie will be missed in Pakistan, they will enrich the lives of people wherever they go. Ken's mind will not cease to be creative and their home will not cease to be welcoming. All their lucky grandchildren will be able to have stories that never end, first hand.

Evelyn and Don Calderwood

Reminiscences and Reflections on an OLD Relationship

From Bob Tebbe:

Ken and Marie became our friends and colleagues when Ken married into the family having served illustrious careers in the British Army and as an employee of Gammon and Co. It could be conjectured, but never proved, that his wise move was in part due to the chorus competition. The Welsh engineers and workers who were employed in the Wah project invited those with excellent voices to audition. Ken's vocalizations were quickly overshadowed and he was put out to pasture as a result. Naturally, it was needful to start over which he did by joining the Sialkot Mission which enabled him to learn to sing the Psalms in Urdu.

I, Bob, really got to know Ken and Marie during my long sojourn and confrontation with Karachi customs on a trip back to Pakistan after a furlough. Laden with boxes, barrels, and drums there was no way that the tariff of three rupees and eight annas could be plunked down to clear the docks with our goods, and also compromise our Mission by bribing the officials. So Ken and Marie provided accommodation and meals at their orphanage while I made daily trips to the Customs House to get things moving. It was a 28-day process and but for the strong support of Ken and Marie I might be there still.

Strategies of British Test Cricket and a huge fish (4 ft. long?) donated for the children's table are memories which are vivid and fresh along with the Espresso coffee brewed up by one of Ken's engineer friends from Italy.

But the most poignant recollections arise out of consideration of the Great Tea Debate which was carried out in the Letters to the Editor of our Mission Newsletter. Ken started it by endeavoring to displace the fabled Japanese Tea Ceremony with a collection of old wives' tales and superstitions about the brewing of tea. These were soundly countered and refuted by a simple statement of the facts about such things as boiling water, gas solubility as a function of water temperature, principles of solution and diffusion, etc., etc. An engineer ought to have these things at his fingertips unless he is using them to test the water temperature before pouring it over the tea leaves. But the whole matter was laid to rest by the brilliant expose of Dr. Wilbur Christy, a layman yet, who was served bed tea by the said Mr. Old in a metal pot and stirred with a spoon in direct contravention of all of his espoused statements about proper techniques for making tea. (I will add, however, that Mr. Old's taste for tea is most discriminating and if you want a good 'cuppa', apply to the said gentleman.)

From Rowena Tebbe:

I first met Marie at the New Wilmington Mission Conference before we went to Pakistan in 1949, and she has been plagued with me as a friend ever since. There is a lot I could say, but I will spare her that and she can giggle in the night about all I didn't say.

A few gems, however, should be shared:

One is Marie stopping by Chitan College to take me to Taxila for the overdue delivery of daughter, Anne. (She had just learned that the doctor I had at Holy Family had been transferred out of the country.) Of course those were the days of slow trains and Marie did not find counting contractions on the slow express from Rawalpindi to Taxila a relaxing experience.

The perfectly groomed little Old boys gave their mother quite a few moments of deep anxiety living next to the frog and cicada loving families of the Stocks, the Tebbes, and the Christys. "My boys are *not* to play in that filthy stream." And what did Ken do when he came? Our kids say he joined them all at the stream. That was second only to the time the Stock kids and the Old boys read about 'Dumbo, the Flying Elephant' and tried to teach the Stock's rabbits to fly! The thing that really impressed Dewey Christy and James Tebbe, occasional 'baby sitters' for Tim and Colin, was the fact that they had beautiful clean handkerchiefs always in their pockets. Marie had a bit of a problem with a popular 'Pied Piper' husband and a raft of kids that loved and were always a part of his never ending stories of the Little People. But we taught our 'gangs' to respect his first hour home before descending.

Cups of tea from china cups, and the best tea at that, warm hospitality, and caring friendship over all the years is the best way to describe Ken and Marie. We miss them still and know Pakistan will miss them keenly. If Ken beats any of us through the Pearly Gates, we know he'll be standing there with his wonderful smile and usual greeting, "Bless you."

Letter from Lucy and Orval Hamm

Soon after the well-known occasion of the Seimen's Company engineer's car accident that landed Ken Old in Taxila Hospital under the care of two stern American missionary nurses, Marie was transferred to Sialkot to help out in the Nursing School and patient care at that hospital. It was during Ken's brief visits to Sialkot that we got to know him, because he stayed in one of the guest rooms of the huge doctor's house in which we lived. About that time our kids also learned what a great storyteller he is!

It was just after we heard that on one of those visits their engagement was being announced that I (Orval) tried one of my unsuccessful puns: Was Marie getting OLD? Much to my embarrassment, she took my joke as a criticism of her AGE!

After their assignments in Karachi and points south, we were overjoyed to have Ken and Marie back in the Mission and we certainly appreciated them in Sialkot.

Among our snapshots we have a picture of five little Hamm kids sitting on a fallen log in the large green lawn of the old district mission house. Ken is sitting cross-legged on the ground in front of them. Like all of Ken's protégés, the kids were completely enchanted by the fairy tale he was weaving which included themselves as the characters as well as other personalities which Ken held in the palm of his hand! We well remember the long wait on the train platform for the *late, late* train which was taking all the kids to boarding school at Murree. The anxiety of leaving home and the boredom of waiting was dispelled by Ken telling a 'continued' story to his boys and our kids.

Years later, when these continued chapters included Joshua Busse, Ken met his most difficult times. He was often interrupted when Joshua would correct him, saying "No, I didn't fly! I rode in a tonga!"

During some of the summers when Marie and the boys were in Murree, Ken and I (Orval) shared summer meals. Ken tried so hard to teach me when to laugh as he shared stories of the 'Punch & Judy' puppets with me! He probably had better luck with 'Punch & Judy', however, than he did in trying to teach me about CRICKET. I still don't understand what 'tricks' of that game have to do with a hat.

And, of course, our house never had the right kind of water, or the best kind of tea, or the right BROWN teapot to make the right kind of tea! Our stove boiled too much air out of the water!

Probably the most memorable times were in the war of September '65 when Ken, living at the hospital, created ID cards for all Pakistani Christians and we gave most of them jobs on the hospital compound as extra security guards. We were without electricity for three weeks and under black-out conditions as well. So we were usually in the semi-darkness at meal-time. Then we didn't have to distinguish between the seeds and ants in the strawberry jam which Marie had left for us! It tasted mighty good in those days!

Ken's experience in London during the BLITZ gave him expertise as well as bravery during the noisy days in which Sialkot was between the Pakistan Artillery on one side and India's tanks along the other side of the city. We all learned to tell the difference in crescendo of the shells approaching us and those trying to back the tanks away!

How we appreciated both Ken and Marie at many times: whether it be our need for technical service, medical help, wise counsel, or property matters. In times of illness or death in the community, in times of discouragement or encouragement, Ken's poetry, or humor, or just good commonsense advice uplifted us all! Keep Pressing On!

We wish that we could just drop in for the weekend and join in the fun, and more especially in the Bible study and prayer time. We miss those special times.

God Bless you all!

Lucy and Orval

Insights from Margie Stock

You two are intricately woven into so many of our happy memories. It hurts us to see you go.

You were the first of our mission family that we met on Pakistani soil when we arrived by ship October 1st, 1956. We were introduced then to the warm hospitality we've never failed to experience in your home. At that time, you were working in construction, but taking responsibility for a children's home nearby. We were impressed by your great love for children—a love that has been expressed in so many ways in your ministry. We understand that you became convinced that Fred would never make it as a missionary. It was because he would not drink the water, only Coca-Cola. We're glad you misjudged on that occasion! Ken himself was greatly frustrated because the myriad of forms he had laboriously filled out to apply to become a U.P. missionary had been lost in the mail! Obviously he wasn't daunted by this, for it wasn't long before we welcomed him officially into the Mission.

Our next, more extended, contact with you was at Forest Dell where for four summers we lived side-by-side with the Norval Christys and Bob Tebbes living opposite. We remember many cups of tea we drunk, sitting on the lovely balcony overlooking the woods, while we talked over the problems of being missionaries and parents. Ken was always the Pied Piper of the Mission. His visits were so eagerly awaited by our kids that we had to keep his arrival secret for a few hours to give him time with his own family. The Wizard of Wozzle, with a twitchy eye, and his raven were important companions to our children in the many adventures Ken took them through. Although he couldn't always remember where the story left off, they never forgot and were breathlessly waiting to hear the next exciting episode. One time, Lois came back from story time with Ken, carefully carrying a fairy on her hand. It was invisible to us, but obviously exciting to her. After playing with her fairy a few minutes, she looked up, laughed, and said about Ken, "That boy likes to pretend!" Some years later an Easter sermon you told at MCS, Ken, touched many hearts and gave them new insights into the miracle of Jesus' resurrection.

I remember you would threaten your boys with, "The last one in will have to eat peanut butter sandwiches!" You shocked your Pakistani friends by reading Greek mythology to Tim and Colin from a book filled with pictures of scantily clad sirens—"most unsuitable literature for young boys."

Other memories of Forest Dell include the time Tim came home from visiting the dairy with his kindergarten class. He excitedly reported, "We saw the cows giving milk from their ulcers!" After reading the story of Dumbo, the elephant who could fly with his large ears, Tim, Colin, Dale, and Paul experimented with the flying capacities of our long-eared rabbits by throwing them over the cliff. We had rabbit stew for dinner!

Early one morning we had an earthquake. Rowena and I slept through it, but Marie and Dorothy Christy rushed outside, came face-to-face in the garden and exclaimed, "Oh, our children!" and rushed back inside to find the earthquake safely over and their kids snug in their beds.

We will always be grateful to you, Ken and Marie, for all you did for Dale. Being dyslexic, Dale was unable to go to college for engineering, and found technical schools in the USA gave very specific training for only one aspect of a job. He wanted to train on a broader spectrum so as to be more useful in overseas work. Ken worked hard to enable him to obtain a visa to attend the CTTC, and mapped out a program whereby he got training in four departments, giving him invaluable experience in those different fields. You also entrusted him with the supervision of major repairs at the Shalom Center in Jhelum where he discovered by experience the difficulties of managing workers and doing construction. This was a stressful, but stretching time for him—excellent preparation for future service. Marie treated him as a son, keeping him in your home over two years as part of the family. We can never adequately thank you for all you poured into him—food, friendship, training, insights, etc.

Your deep concern to help village boys and under-achievers to succeed has always meant a lot to us. You have resisted the temptation to make CTTC more prestigious by giving out higher degrees and catering to boys with greater abilities. We admire this tremendously and praise God for the many village boys, including tribal boys from Sind, who have had the opportunity to get training which will help them make a good living and lift the economic standard of their people. You have also arranged regular times for retreats in Jhelum so that each Christian boy is challenged to give his life to the Lord. God has honored that commitment of yours by bringing many of these young men into a saving knowledge of Jesus Christ through these retreats as well as through the daily chapel times and Bible study classes at the CTTC. We are so glad that Paul has been a part of that ministry as he has worked in the hostels and as chaplain to the boys. He has enjoyed that experience and been greatly challenged by it. We're also grateful that you provided a job for Pat so she could stay in Gujranwala long enough for Paul to win her as his bride. The day they were to be officially engaged, both were experiencing serious doubts stemming largely from the fact that nobody in Gujranwala seemed to be encouraging the match. We asked your opinion and got a favorable reply so urged you to pass that encouragement on to Paul. A few minutes later you greeted Paul with, "You better think things over carefully. You only have two hours to change your mind!" What a help!! However, you redeemed yourself in the excellent way you managed to bring about that big celebration without the secret of their engagement slipping out ahead of time. You also made a great M.C. at their engagement celebration in Murree and gave invaluable help with the 'Punjabi' wedding festivities they had in Gujranwala.

Marie, you have been a wonder in keeping up such a terrific pace over the years! Who knows how many language students you've supervised! We thank God for the meaningful women's prayer group that meets in your home each week and is the powerhouse for healings and transformations in your community. We admire the way both of you can inspire and utilize an unending number of volunteers and short-term young people from such a variety of backgrounds. You are able to provide them with worthwhile opportunities for service and give them invaluable preparation for career work overseas. We are amazed at your ability to use various personnel who have proved difficult elsewhere because of drug abuse, unusual personalities, or other quirks, as well as your gift for discovering highly qualified personnel. We rejoice that you have had the courage to turn over the administration of the CTTC to capable national leadership and have inspired the Evert Lall family to dedicate their lives in creative ministries here.

Your vision for the Shalom Conference Center and all-out effort to put bricks and mortar into your vision, as well as your support of the Golds and other workers there, has created a center that is a tremendous blessing to the whole church in

Pakistan and will undoubtedly be used by the Holy Spirit for years to come. Thank you!

We'll miss hearing again the saga of your ill-fated trip from Hyderabad to Karachi, Ken. We'll miss your enthusiasm for the host of creative projects you have brought into being and still think about starting! Far more we'll miss your fellowship and partnership in the work here. God's richest blessing on you both as you move on to new fields of service.

Lovingly,
Margie and Fred

Remarks about Ken and Marie by Audrey Campbell

Talk about history: I guess my first remembrance of Marie was the trauma she put me thru when supervising language study.

Not too long after that, I heard there was someone reading poetry to Marie, and my thinking about being anxious to meet whoever that was. It must have been a time when they were both in Sialkot.

At any rate, next thing I knew, wedding plans were in the process, and Marie had Dorothy Christy busy acting as 'mother of the bride'. Don't remember if Marie ever used it or not, but she asked me if I had the pattern for a black velvet suit I had when I first arrived in Pakistan. She was looking for a pattern or an idea of what the tailor could make her for her wedding dress.

Many years passed since then—the boys' arrival, both Ken and Marie having very full programs of service and witness in this land. Their real love for Pakistan and its people, especially those of the villages, has been evident during their time in Taxila, then Sialkot, and Gujranwala. Ken continues to have a burden for the boys in the villages.

In recent years, as Ken has become more and more busy, I have been impressed with how he still would find time to help others when they needed it with problems where his experience was useful. For me, it was especially when we first started to consider a building program at the hospital—the advice he gave in the direction we should take. Some people were convinced that the building was not worth putting more money into as it was beyond repair and wanted Ken's opinion of it. Evidently Ken was more for repairing as long as possible, giving a few suggestions on how to cope with contractors, drawing sketches of sewage systems, etc.

My visits to Gujranwala have been few and far between, but I've been impressed with the hospitality of both Marie and Ken even in the midst of their busy schedules.

I'm sure God has plans for both of them as they retire and take up responsibilities in the U.S. — may God continue to use you and make you a blessing.

Audrey

Comments from Barbara

Ah yes, Ken Old has impacted members of our family in quite a variety of ways! Ever since meeting Ken, Barbara now knows that you bring 'the teapot to the boiling water.' Woody still isn't quite sure what that means, but guesses you want to get that boiling water immediately on the tea leaves for the best quality British tea drinking!

Our now adult children still remember Ken as the marvelous story teller that he is. Somehow we recall that Joshua, our one and only son, had the audacity as a child to question Ken about the story he was telling. Suffice it to say, Josh is still boldly asking questions.

Woody is still in awe of the creative, innovative, forward-looking gifts that Ken brings to the work of the kingdom. Ken has multiplied himself many times over through the young adults he has equipped and motivated to use their God given talents for the service of others.

We also still remember Ken's stimulating devotionals before business meetings, as well as his sermon on Jesus' invitation to the banquet table.

Along with all his serious accomplishments, we remember

Ken as a jolly person—the eternal optimist because of his intimate relationship with the Creator of us all.

We thank God for the privilege of knowing Ken Old!

Blessings on him,
Barbara, Woody and all the Busse clan

A Last Letter
from Pakistan

There is a bit of nostalgia in Ken's last letter from his beloved Pakistan. He recounts what God has accomplished and must be satisfied that the Lord will continue the good work that has been started. Although Ken knows in his heart that the success of future hopes and dreams will depend on God and not himself, he naturally wishes he could be a part of it. But he looks forward with anticipation to what God has in store for him next. His life is in God's hands and he will be content to go where God leads and do what God has planned for him. As he has in the past, he will continue in the future to strive to be in the center of God's perfect will.

April 1990

Dear Friends,

There have been a good many of these letters from Pakistan over the past 40 years. This is the last one. Our son, Tim, here on a visit before Mom and Dad retire, especially enjoys the village food. He's now in bed recovering, but it was worth it.

The last church roof is on. For four years I've been working with a congregation on the far side of Gujranwala. As time has passed, I have seen a pastor's house built, the pastor and his family in residence, a church building going up, and finally, yesterday, the church roof completed just before the thunderstorm christened it. I will try to complete the roof insulation before we leave at Easter.

As I look back on our years in Guj I recognize that God has made much growth possible. From 60 boys in the technical school 20 years ago, there are more than one thousand students now on campus. In addition, there are another 1,700 children in village primary schools scattered across the Punjab. This all spells out growth in our Christian community. Our children are getting an education and the help they need to progress.

Next year the first college level class will begin. I am hoping and praying that God will provide the resources to make the dream of a full scale college for Christian students a reality. The new college will provide the upper level of a ladder of progress from the village urchin to qualified educated laity and pastors. It will require commitment, effort, and sacrifice. The capital needed for buildings and equipment, and for the provision for scholarships is going to need much help from outside Pakistan. But I look back at what God has already done among us, and know 'all things are possible.'

What then are our own plans? During May we will be in our home in England. The last weekend will see us hosting some of the volunteers who came to us in Gujranwala over the years. With their spouses and friends, we expect about 50. After life in Pakistan, Marie should be able to handle that one standing on her head.

In June we'll be in Tim's home spoiling our grandchildren. We then plan a leisurely drive across the States to Richland in Washington. We hope to visit as many churches and friends en route as we can. Marie particularly has formed many friendships over the years with folk she has corresponded with, but never met.

How do we anticipate spending our retirement? People here, accustomed to the activity that seems to constantly erupt around us, think we can never retire. Almost daily we are requested to stay 'just one more year'. We had planned to retire to our farmhouse